FRENCHY'S WHORE

*A Teenage Paratrooper
Goes From High School to
the Point of the Spear*

VERNON BREWER II

Frenchy's Whore
Vernon E. Brewer II

Originally Published by:
Windswept Press
Interlaken, New York
1994

Second Printing
Windswept Press
Interlaken, New York
1995

(Third release upcoming: after presented to Amazon for Kindle)

ISBN: 1-55787-121-3, Library of Congress No 94-60593
Manufactured in the United States of America

Second Printing 1995 by Heart of the Lakes Publishing Interlaken, NY 14847

ISBN 978-1-09839-463-9

Dedication

This book is dedicated to the memory of my parents, Vernon E. Brewer Sr. and Mrs. Barbara Ann VanGalder Brewer, who never stopped believing in me.

And to all the Sky Soldiers—fallen and living—of the 173d Airborne Brigade, who contributed everything they had in a place where death was so easy to find and life so easy to lose.

All royalties from the first printing were contributed to the National Veterans Foundation, to aid in their work to help those vets on the streets find their way Home.

A portion of the sales from the second printing were donated to the Sky Soldier Memorial at Fort Benning, Georgia.

CONTENTS

Foreword

Frenchy's Whore represents just one small piece of my Vietnam experience. Writing it has immersed me in one of the most difficult undertakings of my life. Over many drafts I had to fight through solid walls of grief and mental blocks that lasted years. This rewrite—actually its first real edit and rewriting to finally finish what I started so many years ago, at my age of 70 years—was every bit as hard. It is never easy on the head or heart, visiting some of these memories. To write them down is to delve into days, some good and some the dark side of nightmares, over and over again. There is no stopping, no evading some memories, So... like the guys said back then, "Drive on. It don't mean nothin'."

Except ... it really does mean something.

That said, I feel I must reiterate and emphasize that the use of marijuana, though common in Vietnam and all around the world back in those heady daze of Flower Power and psychedelic music, was not universal. Many soldiers did not use marijuana or any other drug. Those that did rarely smoked it out beyond the wire, for obvious reasons. These were years of youthful rebellion and social change. My writing is an affirmation that the soldiers in Vietnam were not immune to those changes. This book is not an indictment of the war or the soldiers who fought it.

Where I could get permission, I have tried to include as many real names of those I served with. For example: Captain Wilson, for whom I carried the PRC-25 radio for many months, who unknowingly saved my life by sending me on an R&R in January of 1969, just before a terrible February 25th on which seven good paratroopers died and many more were wounded. I especially wanted to honor him by using his real name.

I couldn't and didn't know everyone in a company of over a hundred men. Some that I did know have passed on, or died in battle in Vietnam. In other cases I could not find the individuals in order to ask their permission, and have assigned them pseudonyms.

This book is just a fragment of a huge tapestry of diverse experiences lived by millions of young men and women. It might be very similar to or different from the reader's own experiences in that nasty little war, or those in other accounts.

I am thinking I owe a thanks to my old XO in this revision, as he is privy to good info on some of the names, dates and AOs of the revision of this book. Those after-action reports have been invaluable. Thank you, COL Henry Persons…Sir.

I realize that the use of objectionable racial slurs in the dialogue will be very uncomfortable for some readers, and for valid reasons. That said, this was how the men talked in Vietnam. My first duty to the men who served is to tell the truth, not a sanitized version of it. Combat situations and environments do strange and often harsh things to people. I report the words as best I remember them, and ask the reader to understand that including them should not in any way be taken as a modern endorsement of such language. It just happened, and I present the reality rather than try to pretend it was otherwise. I consider that my highest duty—to my old comrades, and even adversaries, of all heritages. This is a true story. I try to paint what was seen and felt. The dates and details are fact.

This will close that chapter of my life for me, I hope; having sought out others who were there with me, and accepted their counsel in correcting errors in the original manuscript, I seek now only to offer sound insight into a world in which the brave young men of the 173d Airborne Brigade lived and died in during this writer's brief time there. This was my Vietnam. I want you to see it, hear it, to feel it. I hope I have succeeded.

Vernon E. Brewer II

Why Vietnam Still Matters

J.K. Kelley

Verne's account might be the most honest, personal, and observant Vietnam story you will ever read. It was for me.

Frenchy's Whore

Late summer, 1968

Somewhere in the rugged Central Highlands of South Vietnam

Alpha Company's Lima and Mike Platoons[1] dug in just before dusk. Their commanding officer had chosen a hill strewn with giant black boulders to set up defensively for the night.

Just before dark, a flood of purple shadows spilled into the valleys as a gentle rain began to fall. The sprinkle quickly became a downpour as their hastily dug positions filled with runoff. In less than an hour the temperature plummeted fifty degrees from a daytime high of a muggy hundred and ten. Around midnight the clouds departed, pulled westward like a giant curtain revealing a black-velvet sky swirling with stars.

Dewey was whispering to Ingland of a girl he loved back in The World when a series of heavy explosions erupted beyond a nearby hill, followed instantly by a crescendo of small-arms fire.

---

1 In the Herd, we used Lima, Mike, and November interchangeably with First, Second, and Third Platoons. The most common US Army usage is numbered platoons and lettered companies, but just think of Lima = First Platoon and it'll be easier to keep straight. I believe the purpose was better radio clarity when there was a lot going on.

Before the volume of automatic fire died down, he raised Third (i.e. November) Platoon's commanding officer on the radio.

Captain Wilson took the handset.

Dewey lay in the mud, listening, as the firing ebbed to a few random shots before ceasing altogether. In the stillness, as rain murmured in the dark, the young lieutenant's voice quivered with excitement over the handset. Wilson's voice was low, calm, reassuring. An NVA patrol had tripped Third Platoon's ambush, freezing the intruders in the eerie, green-white light of trip-flares. The Americans had blown several claymore mines and returned heavy automatic weapons fire. The encounter was over in minutes. Casualties among Third Platoon were superficial; among the NVA, at least four dead.

Captain Wilson ordered the lieutenant to hold the position, to stay alert, to radio situation reports every fifteen minutes. Immediately after stand-to in the morning, they were to sweep the area for bodies, and if possible to reinstate contact with the hostile force. After first light, the two platoons under Wilson's command would move toward the third in a pincer.

Darkness belonged to Charlie. Daylight would bring effective air support and lessen the odds of an ambush. The young American paratroopers huddled in their rain-soaked poncho liners. Staying dry was not an option. Sleep came as hard as the rocks in the mud.

At dawn the men of Wilson's two platoons moved silently off the summit, passing pillars of mist drifting near the trail like ghosts of other wars. Halfway down the hill they entered a fog so thick it reduced visibility to just a few feet. From each man's perspective, the man ahead vanished, reappeared and vanished again amid the stench of rotting vegetation. They moved through dripping foliage single file, at fifteen-foot intervals, pushing toward their brothers in Third Platoon.

Often, they skirted small bunkers dug along the trail; spider holes, they called them. Some were fresh, the dirt around them still red, not sun-dried to the dull brown all disturbed earth turned within hours of being disturbed in this area of Vietnam. Most were rotted, crumbling, dating back to the French conflict. All warned that death could strike suddenly—unseen from inches away. *Just too close*, Dewey thought, staring into an empty spider hole as he passed. *Too freakin' close*.

The sun, almost unseen beneath triple-canopy jungle, began burning the mist off by 0800, turning the rainforest into a sweltering mire of mud, vines and lush vegetation that could conceal an ambush at any given point.

Men cursed softly to themselves as razor grass sliced deep into forearms, leaving thin cuts that bled profusely. A startled troop of monkeys screamed from the treetops, their harsh cries fading as they fled.

One thousand meters away, on high alert, Third Platoon followed blood trails left by the enemy they'd ambushed during the night. They moved stealthily, muscles coiled with adrenalin.

While they pursued, the hunters were becoming the hunted.

Dewey staggered under the weight of his rucksack. Sweat stung the razor grass cuts on his arms as he struggled to keep up with the shadow of his CO. Vines and vegetation snagged his radio, tugged at his legs, sapping energy the way leeches sucked his blood.

Through the exertion, his eyes constantly flicked over the trail while his ears filtered the interwoven music of deep jungle. He had learned the habit of listening for wrong notes. Blood dripped onto the black stock of his weapon and each breath came harder than the last as he slipped through foliage crowding the mud trail.

With absurd abruptness, so close the small force momentarily froze, a firefight erupted: an overwhelmingly loud roar of many automatic weapons firing simultaneously with heavy explosions mixed in. It sounded as if a giant machine were chewing huge metallic gears to pieces. Wilson's Third Platoon had walked into an ambush set up by the same NVA force they themselves had ambushed the night before.

Wilson turned to grab the radio handset from Dewey's hands, establishing contact with the Third Platoon leader while ordering his men to quicken their pace. The nearby firefight escalated into a prolonged skirmish, sending a flock of white birds flickering through thick stands of bamboo and troops of monkeys screeching away through treetops.

Dewey was gasping for breath as the platoon burst into a clearing of flood-flattened elephant grass and splashed into a wide creek, swollen from last night's rain. He thought the grass resembled mermaid hair as it waved gently under swift, crystal-clear water. Fatigue overcame adrenalin as they splashed across the clearing in a near run and re-entered the jungle at the mouth of a shallow ravine. He caught a faint whiff of cooking fish.

As they entered the creek's narrow gully, Dewey glanced down at the bright crimson blood glistening on his arms. He hurried after Wilson, who had left the creek and was back on the winding trail, pulling Dewey along by the handset that was wired to the PRC-25 strapped to his pack. Sweat-soaked curls dripped from under his camouflaged helmet, framing a deeply tanned baby face from which hazel eyes continuously swept both sides of the trail.

The smell of fish grew suddenly strong.

He had no recollection of shrugging off his rucksack before hitting the ground in a bone-jarring belly flop, firing. The two platoons of young paratroopers fought back like a well-oiled military machine, simultaneously opening fire on the left bank as they dropped into what cover could be found. Dewey worked his M-16 like a hose, spraying magazine after magazine of .223 rounds into the lush fabric of the jungle-covered slope. The firing was coming down at them from the top of the bank.

The heavy thumps of a ChiCom .51-caliber heavy machine gun sounded over the high-pitched crackling of AK-47s and SKS carbines raking the line of young paratroopers laying prone in the ravine. A thin sapling exploded a foot over Dewey's head, showering him with moist white splinters. The young troopers spewed a formidable barrage of fire up and down the bank. The enemy was unseen, so no one was aiming. The young paratroopers lay down a continuous field of fire that literally chewed up the upper part of the offending gully bank.

If Ma could see me now she'd have a heart attack, thought Dewey with detached clarity.

A wiry bantam rooster of a staff sergeant scurried down the line, man to man, swatting helmets, ordering troopers to cease fire, to conserve ammunition. Dewey was in the midst of emptying his seventh magazine when the sergeant slapped his helmet. He ceased fire, feeling his legs quiver, his heart pounding into the moist loam. For the moment the communist weapons seemed to have been silenced. The dreamlike spell vanished as he focused on empty M-16 magazines strewn around him.

Dewey stretched out, grabbed hold of his rucksack, and dragged it close. He kept his weapon trained up the gully bank with one hand while fumbling inside the ruck for fresh ammo. There was no more firing from the troopers under Wilson's command, though he could hear Third Platoon still heavily engaged in their own firefight a few klicks away. He refilled empty magazines with one hand using stripper clips, the other resting his weapon over his ruck aimed at the top of the gully bank. His eyes felt telescopic, desperately seeking a target amid the tangled vegetation on the slope above.

His radio crackled with traffic. At least no one called for a medic.

Captain Wilson decided to send out two five-man probes, one from each end of the line, to investigate the top of the ravine. No one seemed eager to take point, so Dewey detached the main bulk of his rucksack so only his radio remained on the frame, then turned to start the climb up the steep bank. A tall sergeant from Texas named Emery fell in behind him, followed quickly by an M-60 gunner between two riflemen. Dewey's senses had never seemed so acute as he crept up the hillside...nor had he ever felt so vulnerable. Spider holes were everywhere. He took his time, checking each hole for movement. A calmness enveloped him as he crept up the steep slope, his M-16 at the ready. This was what he had waited for, had dreamed of: to be the point of the spear. His ascent had no plan other than to advance; to engage the NVA, or to discover that they had already left.

Fifty meters up the slope, the hidden NVA opened fire point-blank on the probe. Dewey hit the ground rolling. Out of the corner of his eye he saw the M-60 gunner and the two riflemen, hunched over their weapons, do an abrupt about-face and scurry back down the slope. The sergeant lay ten feet from him. A meeting of the eyes told each other that neither was hit. Dewey lay in the open, not exactly sure where the firing had come from—but it had been close.

If I move, they'll shoot me, he thought, looking for cover. A medium-sized tree trunk beckoned from a few feet up the incline, just off to his left. Fighting fear, he coiled his muscles then rolled quickly, reaching the tree in a heartbeat.

Easing up against the base of the trunk, he peered around the tree. What he saw sent shock waves through his system. A fresh strand of barbed wire, knee-high and shiny, ran from his tree parallel along the bank, disappearing and reappearing amid thick under-growth.

My God! I'm sitting on the edge of an NVA base camp!

He swallowed hard and edged down a bit, trying to merge with the ground. The sergeant's eyes met his in a silent signal of understanding. Dewey unhooked his mic, trying to break through the chatter clogging his frequency. He could not. All the radio talking among the squads below kept him from getting through.

Then Dewey saw him: a little man with short black hair cut military style, silhouetted by the trunk of a giant teak tree. He wore a long sleeved khaki shirt and seemed to be standing chest deep in a shallow trench. He held what looked like a detonator in his left hand. A drum-fed AK-50 rested on the red clay in front of him.

Though his eyes saw the upper torso of a man in enemy uniform, his mind refused to accept it.

Did they not send out two probes?

Again he tried breaking through the traffic clogging the radio. "Alpha One, this is Alpha One Bravo; do we have any people out front? Over."

Repeatedly he tried to make contact with the company below but could not, and stopped trying. It struck him with clarity: After months in Vietnam he was, for the very first time, looking at the enemy. Not a body found after a firefight, or killed by airstrikes, but a live NVA soldier. For him the enemy had been invisible. Mortar rounds that fell from clear blue skies. Snipers one dodged but never saw. He had seen hastily abandoned base camps, and the tracks of Ho Chi Minh sandals covering muddy trails. The enemy was an animal he hunted as it hunted him.

Not this. Not human.

Yet there he was, unaware Dewey lay less than fifty meters from him. Or perhaps the Vietnamese soldier thought he had killed him when Dewey and the sergeant dropped as the rest of the probe retreated.

Strangeness crept over him as he rested the sights of his weapon on the NVA soldier. All his training had led to this moment. Yet he still had to override a fundamental respect for life instilled by the teachings of a civilized society. *You don't hit your sister. You do not harm your fellow students. You don't hurt people.*

But you must kill your enemy.

Dewey mentally cursed his shaking hands, and saw that the enemy soldier was moving too much, moving his head. He seemed to be trying to get a better fix on the Americans below, moving his head up and down and side to side like a chicken pecking at the dirt. The enemy soldier put down something small and black with his left hand while raising his AK-50.

Dewey's rifle sights blocked out the man's upper body, making it hard to keep his weapon on target. He struggled to control his breathing, to quiet his body. Taking a deep breath, he exhaled slowly and squeezed off a three-round burst as the bobbing khaki torso weaved back into the black of his sights. His weapon barked, kicking back slightly as muzzle flash momentarily blurred his target. Then he was looking at only the big teak tree and freshly dug red clay of the trench. The NVA soldier had disappeared as if an apparition.

"I got him!" Dewey exclaimed involuntarily. Before his words could echo away, he heard the clunk of solid metal striking wood very nearby, then the soft thump of something small and heavy hitting the ground.

The ChiCom grenade exploded against the opposite side of the tree. The smoke and concussion enveloped Dewey, but the tree trunk shielded him from the shrapnel. Even so, the explosion lifted him into the air amid a black and red cloud of fire and dirt and slammed him face first into the rocky soil, breaking his nose.

His world went black. To the other paratroopers along the small creek below, it appeared Dewey had just been killed.

November 1st, 1968

A Rice Paddy Near Tuy Hoa, Republic of Vietnam

The sun shuddered at ten o'clock, a huge yellow gong rung against a cloudless, powder-blue sky. It blazed off rice paddies' water, momentarily blinding a bird-frail old man struggling knee deep in paddy slime behind a massive black water buffalo. He wore only a frayed straw hat and wet black shorts that clung tightly to slim thighs as he worked his paddy, preparing the bottom muck for the planting of rice. The sun beat deep into his back and rivulets of sweat streamed from deep creases on his face as he cursed the buffalo's lineage. An iridescent arc of water droplets followed his bamboo whip as he cracked it against the animal's flank.

"Worthless beast!" he shouted angrily.

The buffalo ceased its plodding. Turning piggish eyes on the man, it shook its massive grey horns, sending clouds of flies buzzing amid bellowed defiance. He had once owned a much better, more cooperative buffalo. Unimpressed, the old man splashed around the buffalo like an angry bee, lashing the animal's flanks with his whip while resuming his verbal attack on the bull's ancestors.

They worked a rice paddy lost amid a sea of paddies, each separated from the others by earthen dikes covered with lush grass. A small hamlet rose like an island a few hundred yards away. Coconut palms, bamboo stands, and banyan trees mixed with litchis obscured a motley cluster of makeshift huts. A few larger, sturdier buildings, their pink stucco walls and curved, orange-tiled roofs pockmarked with signs of earlier fighting, stood in mute contrast. These were the homes of the village elite. The landlords. The mayor.

Colorful flocks of chickens wandered the streets, clucking as they scratched and pecked at red dirt. Pigs wallowed in whatever shade they could find. One lay on its back, grunting in its sleep.

The old man lived in a cardboard shack with a roof of stolen corrugated tin he had liberated from a nearby US base. His wife squatted over a small cooking fire, stirring rice in a ceramic pot with a long wooden spoon.

Until last night a young man, their son, had lived there as well. The Viet Cong had taken him. They came into the village well after dark. Small, desperate men, carrying Russian-made AK-47 automatic rifles, their hard bodies honed by years of jungle fighting. They gathered the villagers in the center of the hamlet. A few lectured them on the revolution and their duties while at least twenty others stripped the village of whatever food they could find. Taxes, they said.

Then they asked for volunteers. Evidently the number did not satisfy the Viet Cong; they dragged some of the older boys away.

Drafted, they said.

But the old couple's only son, just fourteen years old, had eagerly volunteered. When they left with his boy, the old man stood as straight as he could, silent. The old woman wailed for the rest of the night.

The old man did not sleep.

Now he lowered his bamboo whip, his breath coming in gasps. He was too old for this. Once he had a son, young but dependable, and a good water buffalo in which he had taken great pride. He sighed. Such memories served nothing but the waste of time. Though he feared for his son and missed his old buffalo, there was much work to be done.

Still, he reasoned silently, these were very bad times. Much worse than those of the Japanese invaders, or the return of French colonialists.

He had been working this very paddy with his son at his side when a flying dragon had killed his good buffalo. It had come from the direction of the mountains, leaping upon them almost before he had heard its chopping blades. It dove from the sun, its face a blinding reflection, both door gunners firing. He had run to the safety of the dike with his child, geysers of muddy water erupting at their heels.

But it was the buffalo the dragon had wanted. It hovered directly over the frightened animal, sending a steady stream of tracers into the beast. Large chunks of hide and flesh flew from his buffalo as it leaped and bound wildly through the sucking paddy muck. Its legs entangled in its own entrails, it finally collapsed in the middle of the rice paddy, quivering from the impact of bullets and the death now in it.

Satiated, the dragon rose higher and higher until it was a small, dark speck. He watched it fade, far off. His buffalo lay like a black island in the middle of the paddy. A dark burgundy stain spread slowly out from all sides in the muddy water.

As he and his son sat in silence, a calmness enveloped him. He remembered thinking, very clearly, *But it is a very pretty burgundy.*

The provisional government had negotiated with the Americans and he had received another buffalo, but it was a moody, lazy beast. Coupled with his son joining the Viet Cong at the height of planting, that could doom his crop. Pushing aside thoughts of his son, he raised the whip to lash his animal again, then heard something and held his swing to listen.

He turned to the mountains, a wall of emerald green dotted with giant black boulders. The sound grew steadier, louder. He turned back toward the South China Sea, an equal distance to the east. A thousand feet above the rice plain, he saw a small black speck hurrying directly toward him. *Ahhhhh!* he thought, grinning as he shielded his eyes from the sun. *American dragon!*

He stared at his buffalo in contempt, then turned his head and spat a long stream of dark betel-nut juice into the paddy.

Maybe they will kill this animal as well, he thought, turning to slosh toward the safety offered by the paddy dike. *Then maybe I will be given one that will work!*

November 1st, 1968

Heliborne, just outside Tuy Hoa

Dewey sat in the open door of the Huey slick, his jungle fatigues flapping in the wind, a black plastic and steel M-16 crooked in one arm like an integral part of himself. He was engrossed in watching the chopper's shadow, always a little to the left and ahead, slither over paddy dikes to flash across mirrors of rice paddies a thousand feet below. The shadow seemed to be chasing the reflection of the sun which also sped across the rice plain. Always just ahead of the tiny black shadow, the sun briefly turned each blue paddy a blinding gold before abandoning it for the next.

Far below, the chopper's shadow flashed over a tiny native trailing a muddy wake as the Vietnamese sloshed in haste toward a paddy dike. A water buffalo stood motionless, watching the man run.

For just an instant he wondered if the man were a VC or friendly. Then the chopper lurched violently as it dropped several feet on a downdraft. Fighting vertigo, Dewey lunged for his camouflaged helmet as it tottered toward the door. He swung his legs back into the bay and settled back against his overstuffed rucksack, cradling his weapon. Staring down at worn, mud-red jungle boots, he grinned beneath an unruly shock of sun-bleached curly hair that wind-danced in all directions.

Dewey's angular face, darkly tanned and athletic, framed hazel eyes that sparkled with mischief. At least thirty strings of tiny, multi-colored Montagnard beads encircled his neck, along with a leather thong from which two withered objects dangled. They had the size, shape, and color of freeze-dried apricots. Except for the uniform and weapon, he could have passed for any high school athlete.

He peered over at the big, acne-scarred Indian, who still stared unblinking out his own open door. What tribe was he from? Why had the MPs had escorted him onto the chopper back at Tuy Hoa? Why no weapon or rucksack? He leaned back out into the wind, craning his head for a last look at the gleaming corrugated roofs of the Third Herd's[2] rear area. His smile grew as he relished the memory of the previous evening.

Lifting his gaze past La Bah, he stared at the green-blue line where horizon met sky.

America was that way.

Bags of mail and boxes of spare parts separated the two open doors of the cargo bay. Dewey eased back, stole another look at the big Indian. He hadn't moved. With a mental shrug, Dewey pulled his red-stained helmet closer and let out a sigh of relaxation.

As he dozed off, thoughts of home flickered in his head.

Dewey's high school class, who had no idea of his transformation from Vince to Dewey or what it meant, had graduated while he was on ambush months earlier. It had been late, near midnight, as he'd assumed his watch while the rest of the Echo Raiders squad

2 "Third Herd," like "The Herd," refers to the entire 173d. The name originated when the unit was on Okinawa, and a colonel had the habit of playing the theme to the old TV Western series Rawhide.

slept. Crouched in vegetation and darkness, the realization had struck him almost like an inspiration. Goose bumps shivered down his arms.

Right now, he had thought, swelling with emotion, *right now they're walking across that platform and receiving their diplomas.*

At that exact moment, some eight thousand miles distant, his schoolmates were graduating.

Instead of a diploma, Dewey had been issued an M-60 machine gun. He glanced at it on its tripod, barely visible in the moonless night. Even in the dark, the foliage seemed to glow faintly. Eyes probing, he was at once glad not to be with them...but wished Karen Coleman could see what he saw now. That she could see him now.

Dewey belonged to a small but elite unit of paratroopers, the 173d Airborne Infantry Brigade (SEP[3]). It was the first army unit to arrive in Vietnam in the early years of the war. Like all of the airborne, he was a volunteer. Unlike many others, he had also volunteered for Vietnam duty. Vince, as Dewey's parents had named him seventeen years before, had wanted to join the Marines. His father, a veteran of World War II, had backed his decision with a mixture of pride and reluctance, but his mother had refused to sign the papers. So he joined the Army instead, hiding his impending airborne status so she would relent. It worked.

At seventeen, he started months of intense training made almost intolerable by the major mistake of having a paratrooper tattoo burned into his left biceps before arriving at jump school. The Black Hat drill instructors took intricate pains to ensure his stay was pure hell, doing everything they could to get him to quit. At times he was

---

3 This refers to its status as a separate brigade, rather than as one of a division's component brigades. Also, please note that the contraction "173d" was and is specific to the unit even though we articulated it "one-seventy-third."

tempted to do so, but he always found that inner something that allowed him to carry on.

Jump school wasn't easy for anyone. Many washed out in the first few days, but Vince had a motive. No matter how tough it became, all he had to do was think of Karen Coleman. On the day of graduation, while five hundred brand new U.S. paratroopers stood at attention to receive their coveted blood wings, he was fighting back tears of relief.

Paratroopers don't cry.

He made the words a wall between his emotions and his mind. He felt but could not hear his own voice as they had sung; "GORY, GORY HALLELUJAH!", the Airborne version of *Battle Hymn of the Republic*. It was the proudest moment of his life. He had made it with the cream of America's crop. He felt he finally belonged.

The long bus ride home had felt as tough and demanding as any combat training Vince had undergone. Finally, the road sign for his hometown flashed by his window. Empty soda cans rolled noisily from a pile of candy wrappers, magazines, and discarded newspapers at his feet as he rose to collect his duffel bag from the overhead rack.

A familiar apprehension tingled inside him. Although he knew he couldn't be the center of anyone's universe but his own, a subtle tug of abstract thought nagged him.

During all those months of training in distant places, Vince had held onto a scrap of belief that life, except in his immediate presence, ceased to exist. That home existed only in his own thoughts. The fact that life had gone on without him was as basic as it was obvious. Yet somehow, he felt diminished in a way he could not articulate—not even to himself.

Stepping down onto the sidewalk, he set his bag at his feet and basked in the feeling of being home.

The bus pulled away in a noisy cloud of blue exhaust, leaving the young trooper to shoulder his duffel bag.

A green sedan slowed as it drove by. A face he recognized from high school days leered at him, shouting, "Welcome home, Sewer-rat!" The car's driver tromped the gas and sped down the street.

Vince stared after it with steeled eyes.

Apparently some of his schoolmates had no desire to allow him any change of status. Spit-shined boots, bloused khakis, and paratrooper wings made no difference. To them he was still the "Sewer-rat," an evil nickname hung on him by an older, well-to-do boy back in grade school. One of nine children, Vince's clothes were often hand-me-downs from neighbors, and in the peer-conscious society of youth, he found himself fighting his way to and from school. He was the last to be chosen for any game, and had never dated a girl from his hometown. Because of that same peer pressure, they could not be seen with him.

Vince had no such problem in other nearby towns. He was quite popular with the pretty girls in neighboring Waterloo and the camper chicks down at the park. As he grew into his teens and some of his friends started to drive, he found a whole new world existed beyond the stifling borders of his little home town.

"Fuck you," he said, letting his gaze fall from the departing car as he hoisted his duffel bag and strode the last few blocks to the old green and white family home.

His thirty days of leave melted away in a haze of family get-to-gethers and more than a few drunken sorties with his longtime pal, Wild Bill. But there were also moody days of doing nothing at all.

Wild Bill was another of the small town's social outcasts. They had become close because they were both from the same mold: poor parents, wrong side of the tracks, a bitter unwillingness to accept second-rate status. The rich kids said they had big mouths, and they did. But Bill had a vicious sense of humor that he used often, usually on Vince.

Vince was also his father's name. To avoid confusion, his family called Vince "Butch." He disliked the name less than "Sewer-rat," though not by much.

Bill had a way of using Vince's gullibility to put him in embarrassing situations, such as the time he convinced Vince that Karen Coleman, one of the best-looking girls in school, wanted to dance with him. It happened in a small gym where seventh- and eighth-grade students spent their lunch hours dancing to piped-in music and mingling with friends. She had politely accepted his stumbling invitation but had never met his eyes, not even as they parted at the end of the song. She had mumbled a soft "thank you," then blushed crimson and hurried back to the girls' bleachers.

Vince hadn't missed her uneasiness, her blushing retreat, or the rush of tittering girls who closed on her as she sat down in silence. Then there was Bill, roaring with laughter in the midst of a snickering group of boys. Vince apologized to Karen later, but she had said none was necessary. They talked, occasionally, and always wound up working together on door-decorating committees whenever Christmas came around. Though they never did date, they did become friends of a sort. She would always wave in the halls, no matter who was around to see.

Vince plummeted into a one-sided love affair, yet he could only dream of ways to make her his...until he saw how a small country called Vietnam was quickly involving the U.S. deeper and deeper into its civil war. As the fighting escalated, and politicians spoke of "light at the end of the tunnel," he began to fear the war would not wait. That the communists would be defeated before he could become part of the conflict. He desperately wanted to be so. It seemed him to be the one way he could prove to his classmates what he was really made of.

More importantly, it might win him the heart of Karen Coleman.

On his last full day of leave, he swallowed his insecurities and donned his uniform. After reviewing himself in a full-length mirror, he set out at a brisk walk toward Karen's house, raiding a few flower gardens on the way. Turning the comer of Main and Bridge Streets, he almost collided with two frail old ladies. He stepped aside to allow them to pass and they smiled up at him; remembering, perhaps, the young soldiers of their own youth.

Halfway over the bridge, Vince lost it. All his bravado deserted him within sight of Karen's home. He faltered, overwhelmed by years of living what had started out as an ugly childhood joke. Paratrooper wings and spit-shined boots gleaming, he leaned heavily against the bridge's green rail, staring into canal water some twenty feet below. He felt like a sewer rat. One hot sob of self-pity tried to force its way up from the muck in his breast; he shoved it back.

Letting the flowers drop, one by one, he watched them fall until his hands hung empty above reds, yellows, and blues drifting slowly apart. His pride abandoned him to his insecurities as he stuck out his thumb and hitched a ride three miles to the state park on Cayuga Lake.

He found it a pretty loneliness, full of early spring but devoid of people. Flowering shrubs and large trees lined the asphalt paths leading from empty campsites to the main playground, pavilion, and lake shore. Ghosts of children ran laughing over dirt trails that wandered through ancient pines, while the noisy bustle of past family reunions echoed off empty picnic tables as he passed. Today there was only him, crossing the wide grass lawn adjacent to the pebbly beach.

Stopped at the water's edge under scuttling, grey clouds, he thought of Karen with a longing born of despair. A chilly breeze rattled small chains on the flagless pole behind him. The lake's choppy darkness matched his thoughts. Small waves washed strands of seaweed up to his boot tips, exchanged them for other strands, then washed them back out. He stood there for several long minutes, searching inside for fragments of his newfound self-worth. He found only a deep ache. He stifled a sob trying to raise up from his chest.

He felt as empty as the park.

"STAND UP!"

The order, first in a chain of commands given to paratroopers just before they jumped from the plane, rang inside his head and heart. Suddenly he was stepping out into the sky over Fort Benning.

Anger budded, blossomed, then blazed as he raised both arms with fists clenched and shouted to the far shore.

"I'm a paratrooper! Damn it! I'm a fucking American Paratrooper!"

A playful wave swallowed his boots, forcing a small retreat. Another wave chased him farther back up the beach. His anger ebbed as quickly as it came, leaving him with an echo, full of pride but weak from its flight across the lake.

'I'm a Trooper...fucking trooper...trooper...trooper." His echo reassured him.

That night, his last at home, his father handed him the keys to the family station wagon along with a crisp twenty-dollar bill. "Have a good time, Butch," his dad had said with a strained smile. "And get yourself home in one piece. Just make sure you have fun."

Vince pulled up in front of Bill's with a screech of rubber, leaning heavily on the horn. A curtain parted slightly, seconds before Wild Bill emerged from his front door, tugging his coat on.

Reeking of Old Spice and dressed to kill, Bill slid into the passenger seat, slamming the door behind him. "We gonna party tonight, Sewer-rat, ol' boy. I mean we gonna partayyy!"

"Please don't call me that. I got a name, ya know," Vince answered, pulling out from the curb with the tires squealing.

Bill sat back, looking down his Roman nose at Vince as if he were the insulted party. "Sheee-it," he scoffed. "Ya know I don't mean nothing by it."

"Yeah, well, it still bothers me." Vince accelerated to pass an old black Ford.

"Sure, kid, sure." Bill answered wryly, draping one arm over the seat back.

Headlights winked on as cars responded to the deepening dusk. Moments passed in silence. Vince was deep in his own thoughts when Bill spoke again.

"Ya know, *Vince*," he said with a lewd grin, "there is a couple things ya can do fer me while yer over there, soldier-boy."

"Yeah? Like what?"

"Well…the first thing's fer my old lady, so it don't count as much. She wants one of them kim-oh-nos. You know them there dresses the dink women wear that are slit up one side with pants they wear underneath so ya can't see nothin'."

"Done. What's the other?"

Bill leaned back against the passenger door, a familiar *you ain't got a hair on your ass if you don't do this* expression on his face. It was an expression Vince had seen many times before.

"I wantcha tah get me an ear."

The moment of following silence was charged.

"What do you mean, get you an ear?"

Vince knew exactly what Bill meant. He just hadn't been prepared for the cool, casual way Bill asked for the macabre souvenir.

"An ear," Bill said as if asking for a postcard or something, turning to stare out the window. "I wantcha to bring me back a dink's ear. That'll prove to me you were in combat and not peelin' potatoes in the rear or somethin'." He looked down his nose. "Get me an ear."

"Sure. I'll getcha a whole fuckin' head if that's what ya want."

Something cold moved in Vince's stomach as he stared straight ahead, watching white slashes of road divider disappear under the left front tire.

"Get me an ear," Bill repeated softly as Vince braked for a traffic light. In the blood-red glow of the stoplight, Bill's mocking expression looked evil.

Vince returned his unblinking stare. "I said ya got it. So let's drop it."

May 6th, 1968

Cam Ranh Bay

The double rows of uniformed men fell silent. As the plane banked over the South China Sea, Vince took his first look at South Vietnam. It was anything but what he had expected. There were no plumes of drifting smoke, no flashes of exploding bombs. Just a dazzling green jungle that stretched from horizon to sea. Tan sand beaches sprinkled with palm trees appeared inviting, tranquil, almost resort-like.

He wondered where the war was.

After the plane had landed and taxied to a stop, a pretty stewardess stood near the open door, smiling and nodding. Soldiers clogged the narrow aisle and he experienced a sudden surge of paranoia. He had no weapon. How would he defend himself? Stepping through the door was like entering a portal into another dimension. Heat waves shimmered over black, dusty asphalt. In stark contrast to the air-conditioned cabin he'd just left, Vietnam's hot, humid air enveloped him like someone had dropped a heavy, heated blanket over him.

In combat fatigues and wearing dark, aviator glasses, a staff sergeant smiled over a clipboard at the new arrivals. "Welcome to the Nam, boys," he intoned in a cheerful voice. "Step lively now, Charlie's waiting for you."

The soldiers fell into four ranks. "All right," he shouted, "I want all Airborne personnel to fall out and form me four ranks over there." He nodded to his left.

About 30 of the 250 new troops fell out and fell into a platoon-sized formation.

"Congratulations!" the cocky sergeant shouted. "You are all now members of the 173d Airborne Brigade."

Vince, who had orders for the 101st Airborne, famed for its D-Day jump in World War II, turned to the men next to him. "What the hell is the 173d?" None of them knew. Evidently he was about to find out.

In-processing at Cam Ranh Bay took almost a full week. He learned to relax without a weapon, though the haunted eyes of home-bound GIs indicated aspects of this war yet unseen. His days were spent in long lines of fresh-faced soldiers, filling out endless forms under canvas canopies while standing before chest-high tables. Dark sweat stains spread anywhere cloth met skin. Swarms of black flies were a constant bother.

A small group of women filling sandbags around a bunker gave him his first chance to study the Vietnamese people close up. Their speech seemed musical, chirping. Flies crawled unmolested over flat, Asian faces.

Her teeth stained black from chewing betel nut and smoking a dark, crooked cigarette, one older woman shuffled a few steps from the others, dropped her baggy black pants, and squatted to urinate. Boredom apparent on her brown leathery face, she relieved herself as a fly crawled into her nostril and out again. The woman hoisted her black pajama pants back up and rejoined the others, speaking animated Vietnamese while waving her hand toward him. Several of the other women laughed, looking directly at him.

Embarrassed, Vince hastened away.

That same night he was issued an M-16. Guard duty. Visions of a perimeter post melted away as the truck deposited him at the front gate of a motor pool. About the size of a football field and bordered by an eight-foot-high, link-wire fence topped with curling strands of razor wire, it sat alone in the darkness seemingly miles from any other facilities. One bare bulb illuminated the front door of a Quonset hut just inside the gate. Shadowy rows of jeeps, trucks, and personnel carriers sat in silent formation within the wire, while greasy pools of waste oil and the heavy stink of diesel fuel permeated the sand and air outside.

His orders were simple: "Walk around the wire for two hours." He felt betrayed. He had expected at least some danger in his assignment, but this post had all the glamour of a truck stop back on an American Interstate.

Yet walk around the wire he did, relishing the cool security of his M-16, locked and loaded in his hands.

Nothing but darkness and sand surrounded his post, though the lights of the airport and various other buildings glimmered in the distance. He was practically as safe as if at home—but he wasn't home. This was Vietnam, and he was very much alone as he started his rectangular tour around the fenced-in vehicles. The nearest lights were over a mile of dark sand dunes away.

A thin dead tree, no more than fifteen feet tall, crowded the fence at the far end of the motor pool. Barely visible in the moonless starlight, it was the only obstruction he had encountered.

He was directly under its branches when a raspy, Asian-sounding voice screamed, "Fuck Yaow!"

Vince, startled, momentarily froze. Then the voice screamed again, seemingly right over his head. Hands shaking, he swung his weapon up, flicking the safety off and shining his flashlight along the barrel. The few dead leaves and skinny limbs couldn't hide a cat, let alone a human. Yet?

Thoroughly confused, he flicked off the flashlight and backed away from the twisted tree, rifle still held at the ready. The voice did not scream again. After a moment of scrutiny, he continued his rounds.

For the next two hours Vince dreaded his approach to the dead tree. Whenever he came anywhere near it, the voice would curse him in its weird accent until he'd moved twenty or so paces beyond it, backing up with his weapon trained on the dead branches. When the relief truck arrived at the end of his watch, Vince informed the sergeant of the guard about the voice, gesturing with his weapon at the shadowy tree.

The sergeant turned to his driver, trying to speak between recurring bouts of laughter. Finally the sergeant was able to squeeze off a few sentences between laughing sobs: The voice from the tree was a gecko lizard, commonly referred to by the Americans as "Fuck-You" lizards.

Bouncing down dark, twisting, sandy roads, Vince sat in the back of the truck, dejected and embarrassed, listening to the sergeant and his driver laugh themselves silly between pulls on a shared bottle of Jack Daniels. "Fuck-You lizard! Halt! Who da fuck goes there!" the sergeant shouted, succumbing to another round of guffaws.

Their laughter followed him into the wooden barracks.

At An Khe, a 173d base deep in the central highlands of Binh Dinh province, Vince completed a mandatory two-week jungle fighting course. The school updated new arrivals on current methods of booby traps and other guerrilla tactics used by the enemy. Graduation came in the form of actual day patrols and night ambushes set up beyond the relative safety of An Khe's heavily guarded perimeter. On one of those daylight patrols, Vince received his baptism of fire.

His jungle school training squad had traversed the slopes of nearby hills, finding nothing, and was now returning to base. They followed a well-worn trail that snaked alongside abandoned rice paddies, keeping ten-foot intervals between them. A sniper opened up from the wood line, spewing AK-47 fire up and down the trail as the green troopers dived for cover. Small stones, kicked up by incoming rounds, ponged off camouflaged helmets as they returned fire: twelve M- 16s and a '60 on full automatic.

Miraculously, no one was hit—not even the sniper. A sweep of the area found only a handful of spent AK-47 shell casings and bare footprints where the sniper had beaten a hasty retreat down the same trail they'd followed earlier.

The sound of the enemy's weapon was unlike anything he'd heard before. The high whip-cracking sound of incoming AK fire breaking the sound barrier on the way past his head had imprinted itself on his memory. From that moment on, he would react to that sound without hesitation.

He had just learned that a weapon fired at him had a much different sound than that same weapon being fired away from him.

It was dark by the time Vince's plane landed at Tuy Hoa's Air Force base. A truck picked him up, along with four other cherries (as old hands called newcomers; that or FNGs, which stood for Fucking New Guys). Cherries were typically wide-eyed eighteen-year-olds, led around by bored noncoms as they in-processed, then turned over to veteran eighteen-year-olds who showed them the ropes.

His first impression was of sand: acres of it fenced in by rolls of razor wire, minefields, and sandbagged bunkers defending 4th Battalion's rear area. A few hundred yards to his left, metal helipads lay flat on the sand. A half-dozen UH-1 Huey helicopters sat on the pads, ringed by sandbag walls. As the truck pulled away, they moved toward a long wooden building with a wide wooden sidewalk out front and sandbag-reinforced sides. In the darkness, the building appeared to have many doors. "This here's the CQ, supply and noncom quarters," drawled the accompanying staff sergeant. "Y'all take yer orders to the first door 'round back. The good trooper at the desk will give y'all yer quarters assignments. Y'all have a good night now, hear?"

With a wave of his hand, he was gone without a backward glance. Vince followed the others around the corner, passing a closed door from behind which came the muted sounds of a gruff argument.

The specialist fourth class behind the counter scanned their orders one by one, sending each newcomer off in a different direction. The barracks, such as they were, were half heavy canvas and half screening above low wooden walls, all supported by tent poles. Plodding through sand, Vince could barely make out the shape of what appeared to be a large adobe structure sitting halfway between the helipad and his assigned barracks. Beyond the shadowy structure stood sandbagged towers eerily illuminated by floodlights trained on rows of piled-up razor wire.

What a strange place, he thought. As he drew near, voices and laughter leaked out with soft light from the rear of the hooch. A radio pounded out rock music. As the screen door banged behind him, all sound ceased but the radio. Rows of metal bunks marched the length of each wall and support poles reached up from the center of the sandy plywood floor to the rafters.

A group of troopers sat watching him in silence. Vince didn't look at them as he tossed his gear on bare springs of a bunk whose thin mattress was rolled up to the head bar. Leaning forward, he nodded his helmet off onto the creaking springs. Only then did he return the stares.

The throbbing music of *I Heard It Through the Grapevine* reverberated throughout the hooch, along with a scent foreign to him: a pungent blend of burning rope tinged with incense. Sand crunched underfoot as he re-slung his weapon and sauntered toward the silent gathering at the far end.

Fifteen or so young soldiers clustered around the last few bunks in various stages of repose. To a man, their left shoulders bore the red, white and blue patch of the 173d Airborne: a white wing carrying a red sword on a field of blue. Most wore black bandannas and multi-colored beads around their necks. Some wore braided black shoelaces or thin brass bracelets around their wrists. All had their eyes on him.

The odor of burning rope grew overpowering as he drew nearer. A hand slid something under a bunk. It looked like a pipe, still smoking.

"How do, gents?" Vince asked, trying a smile though something seemed not quite right. "Name's Vince. I just got in from An Khe."

A black trooper wearing everything described above and a gold ring in his nose stood up slowly, M-16 at the ready.

"You name's Cid, suckah!"

"Sid? I don't know no Sidneys. Except in Australia. There's a city—"

"Shut up!" the trooper shouted, simultaneously snapping his weapon off safe and resting the muzzle on Vince's chest. "You a plant, aintcha?"

"Well, I am shaking like a leaf." His smile faded into grim, tight-lipped resistance.

Time seemed suspended as the two troopers' eyes locked. For a moment Vince thought of knocking the weapon away. Then another soldier stood up and moved close, scrutinizing Vince's face. Peering over azure granny glasses with bloodshot eyes, a wide, toothy grin crinkled his cheeks. "Sheeeit! This ain't no fuckin' CID man! This here's a fuckin' cherry! Lookey here! He cain't be but fifteen years old!" He spun abruptly and bent to snatch his own weapon that leaned against the wall. "What say we get our young asses down to La Bah?"

Breaking eye contact with the black trooper, Vince saw that the latter's black bandanna had another 173d patch sewn on the back. A combat infantryman's badge and paratrooper wings were sewn above it. The words "HOW YA GONNA BE" were embroidered in white letters along the edges of the V-shaped scarf. A glance around showed that more than one soldier wore a similar bandanna.

The black soldier lowered his weapon. Eyes still burning into Vince's, he flicked the safety back on. "Can't be too careful, boy. Here, or out there. Where you from back home inna Real World?"

"New York. Upstate."

The black trooper stepped back amid a creaking of bed springs as others rose to leave. His expression lost its menace. "You quick on yer feet, cherry?" he asked, slinging his M-16.

"I placed second in the five-mile run back at Fort Dix," Vince answered, stepping aside to let the group pass. The young black trooper followed them, but stopped halfway down the rows of bunks. Turning, he pointed a stiff finger at Vince's chest.

"Ya better be, cause there's only two kinds of soldiers in this here Nam, they be the quick..." He paused, a wide smile growing on his face as he lowered his arm and turned to walk away, his final words slung over his shoulder as if a dare. "...and the dead."

Vince watched them leave, their decorated black silk scarves asking him how he was gonna be. *Quick*, he snarled to himself. *The quickest*.

"So." A voice quipped behind him. "Yer from New York, huh?"

Startled, he swung his head back to the bunks. Three troopers had stayed. Half hidden in the shadows, they looked up at him from cross-legged positions against the wall between two bunks. One, a tall, rangy kid with red hair and blue eyes, stood up and extended a hand.

"Call me Red," he said softly, gripping Vince's hand in a firm shake. "Don't pay them guys a mind. They're all real short. When you get down to just a few days left, well, ya get skittish. Cut 'em some slack. This here's Medlin and Circus Boy."

Medlin nodded his welcome, eyes shining above a half-smile. The other bounded to his feet with a quickness that belied his bulk and soft face. "I ain't no Circus Boy! My name's Mann, Charles Mann! I don't know why you guys always gotta bite me on my ass! Well you kin go to hell, the lot of you! Except you, Vince, welcome to Tuy Hoa." He shook Vince's hand. "I gotta run, my shift's up in a few minutes."

"Man, yer shift was up years ago, lifer[4]," Medlin intoned with bored contempt.

A fourth soldier sitting almost unseen on the floor stood up. "Welcome to the Nam, Vince. Name's Pat, Pat Foglio. I just got here myself, I was in the truck with you coming in from the Air Force base."

Lips pursed and quivering, Mann stared a hole through Medlin, then spun on one heel and waddled toward the door. *How could someone that pudgy make it through jump school?* Vince wondered aloud.

"Shee-it, he's his own circus act," Medlin said, rising from the floor to flop onto a creaking lower bunk. "I give him his nickname. The sucker hates me for it. He's also a snitch, so be careful what you do or say around him. He smokes weed but he'll turn yer ass in to Top quicker'n shit."

"That's a fact." Red said, sitting on the bunk opposite Medlin. "Personally, I don't think you'll need any help getting on Top's bad side. He ain't got but one side and that's all bad. He thinks he's a general; at least he tries to act like one. Him and our larcenous, blub-ber-butted supply sergeant tie one on every night. They inna black market big time. Hell, they're getting rich off this war and staying drunk doing it." He paused for a moment. "By the way, Pat's from Kentucky. Down by the Mississippi and Kentucky lake. Ol' Medlin here comes from over the rainbow. You know, Kansas."

"Yup." Medlin replied, crossing his feet and locking his hands behind his head. "Got here via ruby slippers, been flying high ever since. It ain't all bad, but like the girl said, ain't no place like home."

---

4 Anyone planning to remain in the service for the long term, especially those carving out cozy situations for the long haul. The soldiers laughing at Vince in the jeep over the fuck-you lizards were the first he had met, and the first that taught him to despise their kind.

"Pull up some springs, my man." Red said, shifting to offer room. "Them guys that just left, like I said, they're all short. Me and Medlin, shit, we got beaucoup time. So…where they sending ya?"

"Don't know. They just sent me over here for the night. I'm supposed to report to a Sergeant Greene in the morning. I was hopin' you could tell me."

"Bet on the firebase." Medlin chirped, reaching under his bunk to retrieve what Vince now saw was definitely a pipe.

"And Greene, that's Top. First thing he's gonna tell ya is to stay away from us."

'Yeah, truer words were never spoke!" Red interjected. "We be the baaad boys 'round here. Do you smoke?"

"Sure do, Marlboros. Only got one left though. They were in such a hurry to get us up here I didn't have time to pick up more. Where's the PX?"

Again Vince found himself the focus of laughter as Red and Medlin curled up and laughed until tears streamed down their faces.

"Bullshit!" Vince exclaimed, jumping to his feet. "Ask a simple question anywhere in this fuckin' country and ya get the same response! What is this anyhow? *Laugh-In*?"

"No, man," Pat said, regaining his composure and standing to put a hand on Vince's shoulder. "It ain't. But they do know where you can get some butts. I asked the same question and got this answer. There ain't no PX in the Third Herd's rear area."

"That's a fact, Pat," Red interjected. "Ya gotta go to the Air Force base to find one of them, or anything else of comfort for that matter. Only problem is that it's ten miles down the road. A very unfriendly road at night. All them other troopers what just left here were heading for La Bah, a small Vietnamese fishing village that's not so far from here. It's on the other side of the wire but it's sorta safe. Medlin and us, we all are going there too. Yer welcome to join us if ya want."

"They sell smokes?"

"Bro," Medlin said, jumping up to take Vince by the arm while striding toward the door, "they sell *any*thing yer heart desires."

In the darkness they passed within fifty yards of the adobe-looking structure Vince had seen earlier. He could see now it was sandbags piled atop each other to form a large, square hut. Huge white signs whose red letters spelled out "DANGER! EXPLOSIVES!" and "NO SMOKING WITHIN 100 FEET!" hung from its sides, barely legible in the shadows. "Ammo dump." Red said quietly, noting Vince's interest.

Just yards past the ammo bunker, they turned right in fine-grained sand to follow wisps of tire tracks that ran along the wire and sandbag-reinforced towers. La Bah's soft yellow lights beckoned in the distance as Medlin pulled out a pack of Marlboros, offering smokes to Red, Pat, and Vince.

Zippos flared as his three new friends lit theirs, taking deep drags and holding the smoke in. Vince studied the smoke in his fingers. It looked like a cigarette, but the end was twisted closed. *Marijuana!* This was what his parents had warned him about, what papers from distant cities printed stories about, stories he had read with scant interest. Drugs were as foreign to his little upstate village as razor wire and sandbag bunkers.

I don't know what this will be like, he thought, *but they're all looking at me*.

He flicked his own zippo to life, applying the flame to the twisted end and inhaling deeply. The smoke exploded from his lungs, the coughing fit staggering him.

"Take smaller tokes," Medlin advised in a high, squeaky voice, his own cigarette tip glowing orange.

Placing the filter to his lips, Vince complied, holding the smoke as long as he could. The expelled smoke drifted back into his face, the same smell of burning rope he'd encountered back at the hooch. He smoked the cigarette down to the filter, taking deeper drags as his lungs became used to the harshness. The sand seemed to grow deeper, though its fine grains barely cleared the soles of his boots. It seemed to sparkle like a sea of tiny diamonds.

Giddiness enveloped him. Everything, no matter how mundane, suddenly seemed hilarious. The towers, the sinking sensation of his boots in the sand, all seemed to glow and waver surrealistically. A fuck-you lizard calling in the distance was enough to send him into fits of laughter.

"Feel anything?" Medlin asked.

"I feel great!" Vince exclaimed, spinning once in a tight, dizzy circle. "I want to feel like this forever!" His two friends laughed again, music to his ears. Even the sand seemed musical. Medlin offered another magic smoke, which Vince was glad to accept.

The trek to La Bah was longer than he expected, at least a mile. Before he'd finished his second smoke, the sand seemed to have risen to his knees. Walking became difficult, what with the world swaying this way and that. Finally, after what seemed hours of forcing one boot ahead of the other, Medlin abruptly turned away from the wire, leaving the hard-packed road to stride over moguls of loose sand toward the shadowy outline of a bunker set some twenty yards back in the darkness.

All the troopers he had encountered earlier were there. Some sat on the low, sandbagged bunker. Others lay on the soft sand, chatting with troopers new to him. The fragrant aroma of burning marijuana permeated the area. The men passed glowing pipes around in almost ritualistic fashion.

Following his new-found friend's lead, Vince sat down against the deteriorating sandbags. He could hear waves crashing nearby on an unseen beach and the lights of La Bah had turned into a visible village beyond the wire, some three hundred meters away. He took a pull on each pipe as it was passed to him, scarcely having time to exhale the bitter yet sweet smoke before another smoldering bowl came his way.

"We're just waiting for the MPs to leave the village," Red whispered, pointing toward a break in the fence where two metal fence supports had been spread into a wide V. "Then we'll cross through the wire there."

A path of flattened razor wire, crushed by countless jungle boots in the quest for sexual fulfillment, led to a wide stretch of empty sand sprinkled with broken seashells. Beyond stood shadowy palm, banyan, and betel-nut trees. Pink stucco houses with curved orange tile roofs peeked from the shadows, surrounded by lesser dwellings of discarded cardboard and tin. Soft yellow lamp lights glowed in small windows.

Vince nodded his understanding as he accepted another pipe. Inhaling deeply, he noticed he was sitting next to a black hole in the side of the bunker, a cavern-like entrance. Passing the pipe along, he studied the hole. Tiny grains of sand leaking from an overhead sandbag steadily drizzled into the blackness. He watched them with magnifying eyes and saw planets falling away into a void. In the darkness, he fell with them.

He awoke alone, cold and shivering, his jungle fatigues soaked with dew. Every muscle in his body ached as he clambered to his feet, surveying his waking place with confusion. A bright slice of purplish red colored the horizon where the vastness of a slate-grey

South China Sea met a pale morning sky. Kelp-heavy waves crashed on a nearby beach. Except for an unseen rooster heralding the new day, La Bah appeared deserted.

They all left me, he thought, remembering the planets he watched falling into a void as he had been passing out last night. In the light of dawn, the opening to the crumbling bunker seemed more like a burrow than the eternity it had suggested the night before.

Slinging his weapon, he turned toward the collection of buildings in the distance.

"Could've got my throat cut," he said aloud, trying to keep his balance as he started trudging toward the Herd's rear area. "Just hope Top doesn't cut it anyhow."

Same Day—

Ky Lo Valley Fire Support Base, 4ᵗʰ Battalion

A shirtless trooper stood waiting to greet Vince. "Must be some kind of record," he shouted over the windy roar of the departing Huey slick. "Just one day in battalion and ya already made number one on Top's shit list!"

"Damn! If word don't travel fast in this neck of the Nam! How'd you know who I am and what went down before I got here?"

"You can stop shouting now. The chopper's gone. Aint'cha ever heard of radio? Circus Boy cued us hours ago."

The broad-faced trooper wore the same type of black scarf Vince had seen in the rear. His brown eyes reminded Vince of Medlin, but the resemblance ended there. Medlin was taller with a slight build. This soldier was stocky with a wide, friendly, acne-marked face. Vince fell in step with his apparent guide.

"I'm Vaughn," he said. "Call me Frenchy. You'll meet Iceman and Green at the commo bunker. Where ya from, back in The World?"

"Upstate New York. Small town. Nothing exciting." Vince puffed a bit under the weight of his rucksack and other gear. "Green any relation to Top?"

The stocky trooper laughed. "Nah. Top's name ends in an E, our Green's doesn't; first name Lloyd. Top Greene sent our Green to LBJ for going AWOL in-country. They not too fond of each other."

Vince was sweating profusely. The gritty dust kicked up by the Huey's whirlwind exit irritated his eyes, itched down his neck, crunched in his teeth.

Heat waves shimmered over the sun-baked fire support base, lending an illusion of movement to long 105mm cannon barrels clustered in the base's center. Every big gun sat in its own circular sandbag pit. Large, helter-skelter piles of empty brass casings gleamed in the sun around each fieldpiece. Everywhere he looked he saw red-stained paratroopers. Some were reclining in what little shade bunkers could afford; others were filling sandbags or hauling supplies from the landing zone to various destinations.

The fire base, dug out of the mountainside, overlooked a long valley known as Ky Lo Valley. Alpha Company of the 4th Battalion[5], 173d Airborne Brigade (SEP) manned the bunkers out by the wire while three other line companies—Bravo, Charlie, and Delta—pursued the enemy in the surrounding jungle.

Set deep in the highlands, the tiny firebase was there to provide artillery and mortar support for those elements of the 4th Battalion humping the hills beyond the wire. From the chopper it had looked like a giant, jagged star. A couple hundred yards in diameter,

---

5 For those looking everything up, by an example of somewhat odd military logic, the battalion's formal designation was 4/503/173d: Fourth Battalion, 503rd Parachute Infantry Regiment, 173d Airborne Brigade (separate). The 503rd PIR last deployed as an independent unit in World War II, and the Army used this regimental system to maintain the records and traditions associated with historic regiments' service. Four 503rd-associated battalions served in Vietnam, logically 1/503 through 4/503, attached primarily to the 173d. In the modern era, except for armored cavalry regiments, the U.S. Army has used very few independent combat arms regiments—but many independent combat brigades, as was (and now again is) the 173d.

its squat, sandbagged bunkers manned the points and crotches of the star and each bunker connected to the others by a zigzagging, narrow trench; something to dive into if caught in the open, or to offer access between bunkers even while under attack.

Fire, explosives, and machetes had cleared several hundred yards of jungle around the perimeter. Inevitable coils of razor wire piled atop one another encircled the base. Fifty-gallon drums of foo-gas—a homemade napalm, a jelly-like mixture of gasoline and detergent—lay buried around the perimeter at angles so that only small slices of rusted rims showed. When detonated, the sunken foo-gas barrels belched out a rolling fireball of napalm hundreds of feet high and just as wide. Trip-flares and necklaces of empty C-ration cans attached to the wire provided early warning in case of night attack. From within the bunkers, defenders could detonate scores of lethal claymore mines as well as the foo-gas drums. The troopers on the perimeter were armed with M-60 machine guns, M-16 automatic rifles, and M-79 grenade launchers. They also had M-72 LAWs, high explosive rockets fired from handheld, disposable composite plastic launchers.

Attacking in human waves would cost the enemy dearly in lives, especially factoring in the 105mm cannon's ability to fire either high explosive or "beehive" rounds, point blank. The latter had the effect of a giant shotgun firing thousands of tiny steel arrows that mowed down human waves like a giant scythe.

Then there was the radio, beyond any doubt the most important piece of equipment on the battlefield. With the push of a send button and a few well-chosen words, the operator could call in fire from the huge eight-inch gun back in Tuy Hoa, Air Force jets, Cobra helicopter gunships, or even Puff the Magic Dragon. This was an almost mystical C-130 plane fitted with miniguns and rockets. In just one pass, Puff could shred hundred-yard swaths of a jungle and anything hiding in it. For many a beleaguered paratrooper, Puff was right up there next to God.

Frenchy led Vince across the hard-packed clay, his boots raising little puffs of red dust, until they'd dissected the whole of the small base. Striding slightly uphill he suddenly stopped, turned back to Verne and smiled, indicating with a head shrug his new post.

It reminded him of the rotting bunker back by La Bah, except this bunker was sturdy, the sandbags still green though dusted with the same red dust that seemed to cover everything and everybody. About six feet by eight, it had a small opening in the back side just big enough for a man to dive, crawl, or slither into. The bunker itself was dug three feet into the mountain. Clay from the dig had filled stacked sandbags that made up the sides and roof. Long steel reinforcing bars provided support for the overhead sandbags. Ammo boxes, their tops and bottoms knocked out and covered with retractable canvas flaps, were integrated sideways in the walls at ground level to form firing slots on all sides.

"Gorgeous," Vince intoned, letting his rucksack fall heavily to the ground. "I got me a condo."

Shirtless, still sweating profusely, Verne sat in a corner of the smoke-filled bunker, accepting a white ceramic pipe that was passing from man to man. Although the temperature above ground sweltered at a hundred and ten degrees, it was only 70 or 80 in the bunker. *Still extremely muggy*, thought Vince, *but better*.

Frenchy took it upon himself to introduce the newcomer to the rest of the team. There was Iceman, a very dark-skinned black man from Chicago whose mild demeanor, soft features, starched fatigues, and perfect English seemed misplaced. He seemed detached, remote, almost too relaxed. Next to Iceman sat Green, a muscular, red-necked, card-carrying Ku Klux Klansman from Georgia who happened to speak fluent Vietnamese. A neatly combed shock of blond hair and piercing green eyes completed the contrast between Green and the black paratrooper reclining at his side.

Tree, a tall, thin lad from Idaho, was the only teenage soldier in that particular bunker who didn't smoke marijuana. He wore a simple gold chain with a small crucifix where the others wore beads and scarves. He lay sprawled in the entranceway, occasionally craning his neck to check for approaching danger—not from the VC or NVA, but in the form of sergeants, snitches, or officers, any of whom would gladly send them all to the stockade, also known as Long Binh Jail or LBJ for short.

Two riflemen from A Company's First Platoon, Ingland and Thump, also shared the pipe. Thump took his nickname from the M-79 grenade launcher he carried. Short-barreled and breech-loaded, the M-79 fired a variety of rounds. Mainly used for lobbing HE (high explosives), it also fired beehive and tear gas canisters. When fired it sounded with a hollow *thoomp*, thus the nicknam given the weapon, and often to those who carried it. Thump's squad had long since forgotten his real name. Ingland was almost a mirror image of Vince, with the same short, muscular build, athletically squared face, and piercing hazel eyes. He also carried a radio.

"So, Vince," Frenchy leaned forward, eyes sparkling, "did ya bring any dew out with ya?"

"What's dew?"

"Yer smokin' it!" Frenchy exclaimed, his face breaking into a big smile. "Pot! Herb! Marijuana! DEW!"

"Sorry, guy. I never even made it into the village. Passed out colder'n a mackerel. I thought Circus Boy told you everything?"

"Not quite. But you already answered my next question." Frenchy leaned back against the clay wall, the smile gone from his face.

"Frenchy," Iceman intoned, moving only his unblinking eyes, "She's just a whore. And even if she was not, the Army will never let you marry her. Give it a rest."

If not for the low overhead, Frenchy would have jumped to his feet. Instead, he rose into a tight crouch, glared at Iceman through a drifting haze of bluish smoke, then crawled over Tree's legs and out of the bunker. "You don't know shit, Iceman!" he shouted back into the entranceway.

"Touchy, ain't he," Green drawled. "Hey, Vince, y'all ever have a shotgun?" Before Vince could react, Green reversed the pipe in his hand. Placing his mouth over the glowing bowl, he blew a thick stream of smoke into Vince's face. "Inhale it! Inhale it!" Ingland shouted.

The smoke blinded him, and he did try to inhale as much as he could, but Vince fell back into the corner coughing his lungs out. Green followed, still spewing smoke from the pipe to laughter from the other men.

"That's it!" Thump yelled gleefully. "That's his nickname! I mean looky there! He's in a cloud of dew! What the fuck kind of name is Vince for a paratrooper anyway? You're Dewey! Yeah, that's the ticket! You're Dewey!"

The name stuck. And with that, he had been accepted by these young, psychedelic soldiers of the Vietnam War at the beginning of the Summer of Love.

For the first time in his life he absolutely knew he belonged.

Late July, 1968

Fire Support Base Ky Lo Valley, Central Highlands

Weeks slid into a month. The tiny firebase became as familiar as his neighborhood back in The World. Rows of multicolored Montagnard[6] beads now encircled Dewey's neck. These, his black, braided wristband with its dangling mahogany chip from a claymore pack, together with his black silk scarf, identified him as one of the elite, almost cultist, psychedelic soldiers of The Herd.

All of The Nam considered the 173d Airborne an elite formation. Most had proven themselves in battle as competent, cool-headed fighters. Many, Thump included, had fought in the infamous battles for control of the hills around Dak To; in particular, the savage fighting for control of Hill 875 during the week of Thanksgiving 1967. The Herd had suffered horrific casualties on the slopes of that hill and Dewey was among replacements for those losses.

They were the reactionary force for all of South Vietnam. When something big came down it was The Herd that came in fast, killing and being killed until the enemy was destroyed in place—or, more likely, ran to fight another day.

---

6 A French term for the Vietnamese hill peoples, pronounced MON-tan-yard. Called "Yards" for short by some GIs, often with affection and respect.

Acceptance by these seasoned paratrooper veterans who had survived months of bloody jungle warfare was a source of immense pride for Dewey. In late-night rap sessions, held in perimeter bunkers with troops from A Company or in the communications bunker, his kinship with the others grew tighter than any relationship he'd ever had. In some ways, it was tighter even than the bond between himself and his siblings back home. He had even managed to slip in with Alpha Company's squads for light patrols beyond the wire. Those patrols only whetted his appetite for more of the same.

A diet of C-rations and lurps—freeze-dried meals prepared by adding hot water, designed mainly for Long-Range Reconnaissance Patrols and pronounced like their abbreviation—had melted all fat from his body. The fierce Asian sun had tanned him almost as dark as Iceman. Frequent sniper attacks, though short in duration and generally ineffective in causing any serious casualties, had left him frustrated and bitter. The shooters didn't so much single out any one individual to shoot at; rather, they would simply spray the firebase with full 30-round magazines of "to whom it may concern" AK fire. They rarely hit anyone, but it happened now and then.

One starry night, as Dewey made his way across the firebase, an unbroken beam of thin green light struck the ground almost at his feet. The ricocheting laser was followed by several other bent, thin green beams and the familiar crackling of AK fire. In the darkness, the incoming fire looked like glowing green lasers thrown on black velvet, leaving after-images burned into the backs of his eyes.

That close call was one of several in his first month. Snipers and mortars became standard fare on the firebase.

One scorching hot day, after the sniper had bounced rounds all across the base, Dewey stopped at the entrance to his bunker, watching the firebase return to normal. His rage and frustration seethed inside. He didn't want to believe what he had just witnessed, or what he was seeing now. Troopers were going about their business as if nothing had happened. *Sitting ducks*, he thought, lifting his gaze to the jungle-covered slopes. Hatred blazed in him as he eased himself down into the cool safety of the red earth. He felt as if he were on the wrong end of this war.

Later that day Dewey presented himself to Captain Brown, Alpha Company's commanding officer, asking for transfer from the HQ's commo team to Alpha Company. Brown, tall and broad-shoul-dered with sandy hair and Army-issue glasses that magnified Hazel eyes, responded with a simple question. "Why?"

"I'd make a good RTO, and at least I'd have a chance to shoot back at the bastards. I'm tired of dodging snipers and mortar rounds. It isn't fair. Out there," he extended his weapon to indicate the surrounding hills, "at least a man's got a chance to fight back, to even the score. Here, yer a target for any fuckin' gook what feels like emptying a few rounds into the firebase. And what have we got to shoot back at? Nothin' but trees and brush. It ain't fair and it's fuckin' stupid."

Captain Brown smiled and started to say something, but Frenchy's shouts interrupted him. "Dewey! Get your ass over here! ASAP! We're movin' out! C'mon, shake it, boy. We got choppers comin' in half an hour!"

"Movin' out? To where?" Dewey asked, turning back to face Brown's amused smile.

"That's what I was just about to tell you, Dewey," said the captain. "Two squads of mine and three of you commo guys are being lifted out." He placed a big hand on Dewey's shoulder, point-ed. "See that ridge, the second one back? Well, Charlie Company is behind that ridge, or rather they will be soon. It's a deep valley. They won't be able to transmit out of it. So battalion's setting up a little relay station: you guys. They'll drop you and my two squads on one side of the slope after the Hueys pull a couple of fake inserts. See, if they just dropped you on the ridge top, and that's the objective, then every gook in Vietnam would know your position. So you're going to get in a little humping and play hide and seek. Got it?"

"I got it. But I still want a transfer, Sir. And I'd be damn proud to serve under your command."

"I'll sleep on it," Captain Brown said, chuckling, "but for now you'd better get moving."

The choppers rose out of cyclones of red dust, tilting their noses down as they accelerated out over the valley. Dewey watched the red scar of the firebase shrink behind them, excitement pounding in his chest. Climbing to fifteen hundred feet, the four Huey slicks banked hard, following the ridgeline.

"Okay, listen up!" a young staff sergeant shouted over the chopper's noise. "We're going in on the east slope! First Squad and the commo team will immediately start for the top and dig in! Don't get trigger-happy because Third Squad will be joining you from the other side. I'll co-ordinate link-up!" He turned to Frenchy. "Get set up ASAP! Charlie Company's already humping in! Once they drop to the valley floor they're fully dependent on you guys for radio communication! Thump, take the rear! Wipe out all tracks as you ascend! Use leafy branches, whatever! Stay off the trails! We don't want the gooks to have any indication you guys are on top!"

He smiled, eyes flicking over faces.

"Don't worry, boys! We'll leave enough tracks to keep the gooks interested!"

Pausing, he leaned out the open chopper door and his face grew serious again. He turned back to his men, looking much older than his twenty years.

"You've all been issued extra claymores! Deploy them—but only blow 'em if we're attacked! And do *not* set out any trip flares! We can't risk having critters set one off and give away our position! Okay, everybody understand? Questions? Should be none as I have been over this ten times!"

He leaned out the door again, peering down and to the front.

"ETA, one minute! Last chance! Any questions?"

"Yeah!" Thump shouted. "Which way's home?"

The jungle rose to swallow them. Both door gunners in each craft raked the LZ with M-60 fire, raising dust and shredding foliage. Dewey snuck a look at Frenchy's face and saw stark fear. He hoped his own fear didn't show like that. Tree limbs swept by in a green blur as the small jungle clearing rushed up to meet them. Tensed muscles in his legs started shaking violently. He grabbed his thigh and squeezed hard.

A feeling of things happening too fast swept him. It was the same feeling he'd gotten as a kid when it was his turn to dive off Silver Bridge, or back in jump school as he shuffled to the door, watching the line of disappearing troopers shorten until it was him leaping out into thin air.

He was scared, very scared.

Hanging from the slicks, troopers dropped or jumped as the chopper flared, hitting the ground in a dead run for cover. With a hurricane exit the choppers were gone, a fading throbbing drone. Heart thudding on his breastbone, Dewey had dived into a half-prone position amid the sloping roots of a giant tree. He had flipped the safety off his weapon as he dove among the roots and held the stock against his cheek, finger curled tightly on the trigger guard. There was no incoming fire. The LZ was cold.

They moved out of a stand of tall, mature bamboo into the dimness under the triple-canopy jungle's roof. Here and there, shafts of bright sunlight illuminated slices of lush undergrowth. The smells of rotting logs and moist earth were refreshing after the sun-baked month on the firebase. So was the shade.

It took nearly two hours to reach the summit. Dewey swore silently, a thousand times, that he was dying. Struggling for each burning breath, he made a mental note to quit smoking. His back and legs were beyond pain. They tingled with a stinging numbness.

Counting the commo team, the two squads numbered fourteen, two silent files of sweating, heavily armed teenagers. One squad took a different route to the top than the commo team, leaving tracks to throw off any discovery by the NVA. The team Dewey was with bypassed several trails on the ascent, keeping to beds of moss, rocks and, when necessary, tangles of vines and brush a rabbit couldn't have worked through.

The crest of the ridge was a pleasant surprise. Chest-high grass dotted with large rocks provided good cover and formed a natural, diamond-shaped LZ thirty yards across at its widest point. It had also been a Viet Cong base camp, months earlier. The bunkers had overhead cover of logs and dirt that showed signs of early decay and were dug into the most logical defensive positions. Charlie knew his business, most of the time.

The west side of the ridge dropped off as a sheer cliff of black rock for a thousand feet, leaving only narrow necks of the ridge and the steep east slope to defend. There was a large command bunker centrally placed back in the weeds. Thick grass grew from the roof of dirt piled atop layers of mossy logs. Frenchy claimed it for the commo team. He had the relay station functional in minutes, establishing contact with the firebase and all other squads from Lima Platoon.

Third Squad found the west slope a difficult, much steeper ascent. Their team leader, his words coming in gasps, radioed they'd have to move along the ridge a klick or two before starting uphill again. That placed them in a bad spot, forcing a choice between abandoning stealth for speed, or spending the night on the slope. They opted to join the others on the top, barely making it.

Fuck-you lizards and fireflies were already making their presences known when a soft whistle came from the ridge just beyond the grass. A raspy voice on the radio asked if they'd been heard. Frenchy received an affirmative from the perimeter before whispering clearance.

The last squad staggered into the clearing in single file, each man bent under the weight of his full rucksack. Before total darkness, their defenses were complete. Fuck-you lizards cursed the night all around them.

Dewey's shift began at two A.M. Charlie Company had not yet reached the narrow floor of the gorge but had set up numerous ambushes the length of the small valley. With one of two PRC-25s set on C Company's frequency, Dewey was privy to the periodic situation reports between widely separated ambush sites. Nothing transpired. All reports were negative. In response to sit-rep requests, twice-broken static from each site's radios confirmed lack of contact. Had any site broken squelch only once, it would have meant visual or audible contact with the enemy.

Breaking squelch was SOP throughout the brigade, enabling troopers to communicate their status with silent squeezes of the send button on their radio handsets. Even whispered reports might give away U.S. positions. Dewey's own situation-report requests were answered silently, negatively. Sit-reps were called for every fifteen minutes, to radios tuned so low only the man on guard could hear.

Half an hour before dawn, all troops on the tiny perimeter were awake for stand-to. No one smoked or spoke above a whisper for half an hour. Then the soft aroma of brewing coffee and burning tobacco drifted in the cool morning mist.

For a week they stayed on line, waiting to be needed by Charlie Company, but for reasons unknown the firebase was receiving all Charlie Company's transmissions clearly back at the firebase. No relay had been needed, yet; or so command suggested. They were to stay on line until told otherwise. Boredom, relieved only by a resupply chopper kicking out cases of C-rats like bombs in low, full-tilt-boogie fly-bys, became the real enemy.

Dewey cut fifty-two rectangles of thin grey cardboard from C-rat boxes. Pen in hand, he spent hours creating a passable deck of cards. That same afternoon he lost $350 playing acey-deucy with Ingland and several of the other men. Signing a promissory note over to Fyle, a rifleman from Third Squad, he gave up the game and went to join Thump and Ingland at their small bunker on the south end of the ridge.

Sparks cascaded from the fuming pipe as a seed exploded, several finding their way inside Dewey's fatigue shirt. He quickly beat them out. A soft breeze wafted the smoke over the grass where it dispersed beyond the cliff rim. "Got to watch them seeds." Ingland said. "Hot little suckers burn to the bone. And they don't go out until you put them out."

"Speaking of out. When they gonna get us off this gawd-fer-saken ridge?" Thump asked, turning to Dewey, who just shrugged.

"Hey! Don't knock it!" Ingland answered. "We might get lucky and stay here 'til we DEROS. This beats slinking down gook trails in broad daylight. Ain't no booby-traps or ambushes to worry 'bout. Shit, man, we got it dicked up here."

The sun was dying in a sea of purple and orange over the mountains when a firefight erupted in the valley below. Dewey dived into the commo bunker where Frenchy was hunched over a radio. He jerked a hand up to silence Dewey's questions.

"Charlie One, this is Charlie Mike-Two-Four!" an excited, unfamiliar voice shouted over a background of explosions and automatic weapons fire. "We got four down VC! Looks like they were point for battalion! Taking RPGs and heavy small arms. Request marker smoke at Charlie One-Six, Bravo Two-Zero-Niner, over!"

"This is One!" Dewey recognized the voice of C Company's CO. "Roger that. Willie-Peter en route! Standing by. Over."

A single 105-millimeter round shrieked overhead, exploding in a greenish-white blossom on the narrow valley's far slope. Green tentacles arched from the explosion, trailing white smoke as they fell back to the jungle.

"Yes! That's it! That's it! Battery fire for effect!"

The 105s back at the firebase thundered. Seconds later, HE shells shrieked over the relay station, exploding in a cluster of black and red fireballs precisely where the marker round had impacted. The firing continued for ten minutes, shrieking rounds impacting up and down the slope as directed by Charlie Company's artillery FO[7] until a haze of dust and smoke drifted over the jungle.

Charlie Company's Second Platoon had walked into a point element of North Vietnamese regulars. The point man had spotted them quickly enough to set up an impromptu ambush, thinking them a small patrol, not point for a battalion. The four NVA died instantly in a hail of M-60 and M-16 rounds, but the huge volume of return fire had caught the Americans completely off guard.

---

7 Forward Observer. A soldier with special training in calling for artillery and air support in all forms.

Two Charlie Company troopers lay dead as the platoon swept the jungle the 105s had ravaged. They found several Russian-made AK-47s and numerous blood trails, but no more bodies.

Half the men on the ridge had gathered around the commo bunker to follow the firefight, and a stifled cheer went up as the actual body count mounted to twelve dead North Vietnamese. The slapping sounds of chopper blades silenced the celebration as a Huey slick, wearing huge red crosses painted on white backgrounds over the closed doors, swept over the ridge and dropped into the valley. The medevac beelined toward a plume of purple smoke rising from the green canopy covering the valley floor.

That night Dewey joined Ingland and Thump on the perimeter, wearing a cloth bandoleer of full M-16 ammunition magazines and his utility pockets crammed with grenades.

"Bad shit inna air," Thump said quietly. "I can feel it."

The bunker, with its overhead protection of moldy logs and grass-covered earth, was barely large enough to hold two men, so Dewey sat in the shallow trench Ingland and Thump had dug across its entrance. Plastic detonators for claymore mines lay in sequence on a log they'd placed in front of their position. Thin black wires ran from the firing mechanisms down the slope, disappearing in different directions a few feet beyond the log.

Thump pulled his poncho over his head to light a bowl. "I wouldn't," Ingland whispered.

"I would," came the muffled reply.

With utter disbelief, Dewey watched a claymore detonator vanish as if it had never been there. Another one followed the first before he had time to react.

"Gooks!" he hissed in a loud whisper as he grabbed for the third detonator. Something yanked it from his fingers. Thump was shrugging off his poncho and Ingland dove for his weapon as Dewey grabbed the last detonator and squeezed.

The blast lit up the slope some twenty meters away. Dirt and debris fell among them as Dewey emptied his pockets, pulled the pin from a frag, and threw it downhill in a hard, high arc. He quickly repeated the process until he'd lobbed several grenades randomly down the slope. More explosions shattered the darkness. In brief flashes of fire he saw figures running parallel to their positions. Other claymores were blown down the line and many more frags exploded on the slope before quiet returned to the night.

Even the fuck-you lizards quit cursing. No one fired their weapons. The explosions were bad enough, but muzzle flashes or tracers would give away their exact positions.

No return fire or other activity came from below as they waited in tense, silent groups. Only frantic whispering over the radios made any sound at all.

Dewey didn't sleep that night. After stand-to the next morning, he joined Ingland's squad for a sweep of the slope. They started down the ridge in single file until they'd flanked the area where they saw the movement the night before. Using hand signals, the line turned to the right and began the sweep, weapons at the ready.

"Damn!"

The shout froze Dewey in his tracks.

"Over here!" The voice belonged to Turner, Second Squad's M-60 gunner. "Holy shit! What a friggin' mess!"

The troopers quickly converged on Turner, who stood atop a large black boulder. His sixty was lowered and he shook his head in obvious disgust. As the first troopers drew near, he pointed at the ground in front of him with the muzzle of the M-60.

A large charcoal-gray ape, claymore wires wrapped around its legs, lay dead alongside the boulder. Blood matted its long hair and a frozen snarl bared yellowed canines over an inch long. Pieces of other apes littered the slope.

"Rock apes," Turner muttered to himself. "Friggin' rock apes."

The search turned up seven dead apes of various sizes, and pieces of several more. Swarms of flies and armies of ants were already hard at work on the remains before all the claymore mines were untangled or replaced.

Dewey stopped at Ingland's bunker for a few tokes on a pipe and some good-natured ribbing before dragging himself over to the commo bunker and falling asleep on a poncho liner in the hot sun.

Iceman shook him awake. Dewey sat up instantly, reaching for his weapon. "Chill out, Dewey. You have to pack up. We're being extracted."

"Where to?" he asked, rubbing sleep from his eyes.

"They say the rear," Iceman answered. "I'll believe that when I see La Bah."

"La Bah." Dewey sighed. "Such a nice name, La Bah. Are the whores really as good as I've heard?"

"Better. If you like your woman flat-chested and slant-pussied."

"Sheeit!" Dewey shot back as he folded his poncho liner. "That's a myth. All women look alike if ya turn 'em upside down."

"Okay," Iceman smiled, his gold tooth glinting in the sun, "you wait and see. They may not be slanted but I've seen more hair on a bowling ball."

"As long as it's wet-n-warm!" Dewey chuckled. "I got no prejudices."

Iceman glanced over at Frenchy. Busy packing radio gear, he wasn't following their conversation. Even so, Iceman lowered his voice. "There is one girl there you should know about," he said, leaning close to Dewey's ear. "You won't be able to miss her, she's got a face like an abused potato and smells like rat piss mixed with nuoc-mam[8]."

"Thanks for the advice. I'll try to control myself."

"Listen, I'm serious. She's also got the only set of real tits at Mama-San's East. They're perfectly formed, stand up all by themselves, and she wears see-through shirts. Man, it's a sight for sure... but leave her be."

"Well, not that rotten potatoes and smelly women don't turn me on, but why all the concern?"

"Frenchy." Iceman said, stooping to pack his own ruck. "He wants to marry the wench and I do believe he'd shoot anyone he found in bed with her."

"He's got it that bad, huh?"

"Or that good. I guess it depends on your point of view."

"Wellll," Dewey sighed, sitting on his rucksack, "In light of her description, I'd have to say it be a severe case of a lack-of-view."

Leaning forward, Dewey picked up his helmet. Studying the peace sign drawn with black magic marker on its side, he reached in his shirt pocket and took out a pen. Very slowly, very precisely, he drew seven small monkeys in a row. Holding the helmet up, he called over to Iceman, indicating the row of penned-on monkeys. "Yo! Lookey here! This enough monks to make me an ace?"

---

8 Pronounced 'nook-mom,' this strong-smelling, salty anchovy sauce is a favorite Vietnamese condiment. Some US soldiers acquired the taste, but all recognized the odor.

That afternoon they were abruptly pulled off the hill. The relay station never had been necessary. Now they were returning to the firebase, plucked from the field by a brace of Hueys.

Just before they left the hill, Dewey picked up a radio transmission from HHQ. A new company was being added to each battalion, to be called Echo Company. In reality, E Company would never be more than a reinforced platoon in strength. What got Dewey's intense attention was that there was a call out for volunteers. His MOS as an RTO was in demand. Without seeking permission, he wasted no time catching a slick for the rear at Tuy Hoa. Dewey thus became among the first incorporated into Echo Raiders, the new recon platoon for the 4th Battalion. One of his buds from the Commo platoon, a young trooper from California named Session, had also volunteered.

For the next three weeks Dewey lived his dream, humping the boonies with Echo Raiders as a paratrooper with the 173d Airborne Brigade. The mission was recon in force[9]. In those three weeks, working the highlands with troopers from all four companies of the 4th Battalion, the young veterans of the famous battles in the hills around of Dak To taught Dewey the principles of jungle warfare. He was a quick study, learning how to stay alive and in one piece while avoiding booby traps, bamboo vipers, punji sticks, and leeches. He was taught to carry only what he absolutely needed or was ordered to. Humping up and down jungled slopes taught him to discard the Army-issue boxer shorts, which rolled up each leg and put a stranglehold on his family jewels. He did not wear boxer shorts again for the rest of his tour.

---

9 A reconnaissance in force is a reconnaissance mission that is intended to test enemy strength, readiness, force composition—in many cases, by firing the enemy up and seeing what happens. This is called "recon by fire." All recon in force was actually just another term for "Search and Destroy."

Three weeks of uninterrupted humping of the Central High-lands' jungle-covered slopes melted any fat off Dewey's frame and hardened him with the weight of an 80-pound rucksack. He proved a quick study at walking point, which was a dangerous job indeed. Although enemy contact was rare in those weeks, he learned the smell of his enemy: a kind of stale sweat, cooking fish smell, one that would raise the hairs on his neck. He learned to spot thin wires strung across the trails, and that it was sometimes good not to use those trails, especially if those trails were covered with what looked like tire treads—the tracks of Ho Chi Minh sandals, made from ac-tual salvaged tires. Dewey came to understand that forcing a platoon through the jungles off those trails meant back-breaking work, but that when speed was essential, the trails were worth the risk.

In one instance, while working the area around Duc Lap Spe-cial Forces camp outside of Buon Ma Thuot, Echo Raiders found a bamboo hooch full of hand-carved and beautifully hand-painted teak wood crossbows. They were too big to carry for souvenirs; as they would catch on every vine and limb, there was no way to carry them, and no way to send even one home from the jungle. Dewey damn near cried when they burned the hooch with a hundred works of crossbow art inside.

They also discovered a race of indigenous people, new to them, living in the jungle-covered mountains in that AO[10]. These were Rhade tribesmen, Montagnards. The ethnic Vietnamese called these indigenous people "Muy," which translated into "savages." No love was lost between the Rhade and either Vietnamese side in this war, but the NVA had gotten to some Rhade villages years ear-lier, promising autonomy in exchange for their fighting for the com-munist side. Some did; some did not. Fiercely independent, most of the "Nyards" fought against everyone except their own tribe.

---

10 Area of Operations.

One day while on point, Dewey encountered an intricately woven bamboo wall, waist high, with short thin bamboo bent into U-shapes woven into the wall every ten feet, creating small doorways a foot or so high. Bent saplings on either side of the doorway held snares. The wall went on for hundreds of meters. A trapper himself in his younger days, Dewey was more than impressed. To his disappointment, there was not opportunity to explore just how far this wall of snares went.

The enemy's ability to craft hazards was a wonder. On one extremely hot and humid day, Dewey was breaking brush on a vine-overgrown, long-disused trail. He swung his machete with purpose, hacking at an almost solid wall of vegetation. Sweat dripped down his brow into his eyes and off his nose. In the middle of one swing, Dewey saw movement out of the corner of his eye: a bush abruptly swaying back and forth in the hot still air. Using hand signals, the column stopped while Dewey and several other troopers flanked the moving bush by approaching it using the cloverleaf patrol method[11]. They discovered the first of several booby-trapped "spear chutes" found that day. Each was a ten-foot-long section of thick bamboo three inches wide, cut in half lengthwise, forming a chute fixed onto a platform of stakes holding an eight-foot-long bamboo spear sharpened to a needle point. A wrist-thick sapling, tied down with a vine located just where a boonie rat might hack with a machete, was the trigger. The whole giant crossbow was aimed precisely where Dewey had been standing while hacking at the vines.

On examination, they discovered that one of the vines Dewey had cut was tied to the sapling that had grown into the bent-over position in which it had been left, perhaps a year or more ago. The sap-

---

11 Approaching the objective from several different angles, describing circles much like those of a three-leaf clover.

ling had been inserted into a notch on the blunt end of the spear. A year earlier, the sapling would have launched the spear through the spot where Dewey had stood cutting the triggering vine with his machete. He found three more just like it before the day was through. Later that evening, via the radio, they learned a Charlie Company trooper had not been so lucky. He had cut into a fresh booby trap that launched its spear through both cheeks of his ass.

That all came to an end after just three weeks when any and all troopers of Echo Raiders not carrying an 11B MOS[12] were called back to An Khe under the guise of being trained for that MOS, when in reality the powers-that-were assigned them to some NCOs that were building a water tower on the Herd's rear area. Dewey went out on a couple of NCO-sanctioned raids to steal materials from the 1st Cav, but crawling around in the darkness and loading trucks with stolen steel right under the noses of armed guards did not appeal to him. So he again left that assignment without permission, and caught a Caribou at Tuy Hoa airbase that was flying to Duc Lap. Upon arrival, an NCO from the Commo team cornered him and forced him to join Pat Foglio and another fellow 173d RTO, Jack Kranchick, atop Duc Lap Special Forces camp to relay messages from field troops whose localities did not permit them to call for support or resupply. Jack, a tall good-looking sergeant who had control of the commo team beyond the wire, came from the hills of Pennsylvania. He did not partake of marijuana, but there was no way he could have missed its use. The guys considered him a solid paratrooper, and respected him enough that they refrained from smoking dew in front of him.

---

12 Usually expressed as "Eleven Bravo," sometimes "Eleven Grunt." The Military Occupational Specialty of Infantryman; simply put, a rifleman experienced with all the weapons in the infantry arsenal.

Their duty station atop the blasted red mud of Duc Lap was a long, narrow bunker, only four feet high inside and dug deep into the hillside—a hillside that had been overrun by thousands of NVA just days before. The Special Forces team had held out, mainly in one bunker up top, while artillery and bombs dropped by fast movers[13] had plowed the NVA and the hill under, leaving a moonscape of red mud quickly turning that familiar reddish brown that eventually stained all personnel and equipment. With so much explosive ordnance hitting the hill from all sides, the bunkers' top layers of sandbags had been pulverized, leaving only the bunkers' entrances to indicate their positions.

US forces had only recently retaken Duc Lap and relieved the hard-pressed Green Berets holding out in the main bunker they had named "The Summer Cottage." A small, hand-painted wooden sign proclaimed the bunker as such. It was like a bar inside—a real bar, with a mirror behind it, well stocked with bottles of whiskey. It even had a small TV above it in one corner. Foglio, Kranchick, and Dewey spent ten days up there, dodging incoming and living with the huge rats that also called those bunkers home.

One afternoon, Dewey was sitting outside the bunker watching two Cobra gunships make minigun and rocket runs on the jungle below them about five miles to the south. He could see the gunships actually stutter-recoil from their weapons firing, but it took several seconds for the sound of the miniguns and explosions of rockets to reach his ears.

Suddenly one of the Green Berets ran over to him from the direction of the Summer Cottage bunker, shouting for Dewey. "Get them off us! They're hitting our troops!"

---

13 Jet aircraft.

"I don't have the frequency! I don't know whose gunships they are!" replied Dewey.

The soldier turned and ran back to the bunker he came from. Dewey got on the radio and called down to Battalion Command, asking whose gunships they were. The other voice told him they were attached to the 4th Infantry Division. He dropped the handset and ran over to the Summer Cottage. Bursting through the sunken door, he saw four Green Berets huddled around a huge stack of radio equipment and could hear a frantic voice screaming: "Cutty Sark One, this is Cutty Sark Two! Get them off us! Oh, Christ! They're making another pass!" Also very audible in the transmission was the sound, now in real time, of the Cobras' stuttering miniguns and the heavy explosions of 2.3mm rockets from its pods.

Dewey shouted that the Cobras were with the 4th ID, but the SF men waved him away in frustration. They had already ascertained that fact. Half stunned, Dewey walked back up the steps cut into the red clay to the bright sunshine beating down on the summit of Duc Lap. Plodding over to his own bunker, he saw Foglio sitting on sandbags watching the distant gunships orbiting high above the jungle where smoke rose up from their earlier passes. Within minutes, a flight of four medevac Hueys passed over them, making bee-lines for the smoking area of jungle. Ten minutes later they returned overhead, flying fast and overloaded with wounded Montagnards.

Dewey never knew the fate of the wounded Cutty Sark Two, only that he had been gut-shot.

The next day, while sitting atop his bunker reading a letter from home, Dewey heard the heavy "whumpf" of a large mortar tube. Looking up from his mail, he watched hot gases erupt from behind the fourth row of banana trees in the plantation at the foot of the hill. He could actually see the projectiles' blurred ascent, but was helpless to do anything about it. The mortars landed in an open field between the camp down below and the base of the hill. No one seemed to pay any attention to what was obviously incoming fire and Dewey, armed with just an M-16, had no way of attacking the mortar's crew. It was well within range of his rifle, but only four rounds came in, all landing harmlessly. He could not take the chance of firing on a position when he had no idea who was dropping the mortars. It would seem an open case of enemy fire, but no one else was doing anything, so neither did he…for the moment.

The first chance Dewey got, he sought out the new Alpha Company commander, Captain Wilson, asking to become his personal RTO. Wilson had replaced Captain Brown, who had died in an NVA sapper attack on Fire Support Base Lance on 7 September 1968.

Dewey would later learn the full details about that awful night on Firebase Lance from other Alpha troopers who had endured the attack including DeGrau, Oliphant, Hopkins, and Chuck Dugo. These were men he knew from back on the firebase in Ky Lo Valley and on the trails. These were Brothers, period.

Dugo, an Alpha Company survivor of the attack, might have been one of the luckiest men in The Nam. Gravely wounded at the firebase, the medics had at first pronounced him KIA. They wrapped him in a poncho—the field substitute for a body bag—and sent his "remains" out on a medevac with nine other KIAs. Only when his body reached Graves Registration did someone hear him moaning and realize that Dugo was still alive. As best the doctors could determine, the rough chopper ride had been his salvation. The bodies stacked on top of him, bouncing with the turbulence, had performed crude but effective CPR.

All but one ranking officer believed Alpha Company had done a superb job of reacting to a well-planned and executed night attack. The NVA had studied the base for a month while it was held by Charlie Company. On the day Captain Brown's Alpha Company moved in to take over security for the firebase, he called a meeting of platoon leaders to discuss likely avenues of attack from the surrounding jungle. He pointed out a flat area of higher ground that led right into the level portion of the base. "This is where they will try to come in," he had stated—and he'd been correct.

That was exactly where the sappers had penetrated the base, using homemade Bangalore torpedoes. The NVA filled a ten-foot length of bamboo with plastic explosives, then screwed more lengths of bamboo into it so they could slide the explosives into place. This avoided the trip flares, passed the wire without tinkling any cans, and enabled the sappers to shove the business end of the torpedo into the bunker's gunport. Its detonation would destroy the bunker, killing or maiming all inside, thus giving the NVA an opening to enter the camp. Some of the NVA sappers were suicide bombers and leaped into bunkers with satchel charges strapped to them, with similarly lethal results.

DeGrau and Hopkins had been about a hundred meters beyond the wire at an LP[14] when the Bangalore torpedoes took out the first bunker. Seeing what was going on, they tried to warn the base, talking softly on their radio while NVA soldiers were scrambling within mere feet of them. The first explosion in a bunker sent a chunk of hot steel through a PRC-25 radio, keying the mic, so no one could transmit on that frequency—one shared by all of Alpha Company.

DeGrau knew he had to get back inside the wire, but was concerned about being mistaken for the enemy. He also knew that there were NVA inside the wire killing his buddies, so he took the chance. He sprinted toward the perimeter, staying low, exposed in the

---

14 Listening post.

brief light of explosions, yelling at the top of his lungs: "DO NOT SHOOT US! AMERICANS! G.I.S COMING IN!" Passing the wire via a blown bunker, he almost ran into two of the NVA sappers, wearing only shorts, escaping at a dead run. Without breaking stride he killed both with a burst from his M-16. Other sappers did escape, but not many; they left 15 dead by body count, but managed to drag away some of their dead and wounded. Counting Dugo, the 173d had suffered ten KIA, that number dropping to nine when Chuck Dugo turned up alive at Graves Registration.

With Alpha understrength, and a stint with Echo Raiders under Dewey's belt, he presented his RTO services to Captain Wilson. The commander accepted, and Dewey relished the opportunity to take his place with a combat element of the 173d.

October 31st, 1968

Tuy Hoa, Rear Area of the 4th Battalion

Even with the canvas sides of the wood-frame hooch rolled up, it was hot and muggy inside. No breeze stirred where Dewey stood staring, as if possessed, into an outrageous sunset palette-knifed over distant blue highlands. Molten orange and violet clouds crawled along the highland's spine, setting fire to rice paddies halfway to the sea. Monkey Mountain, a massive peak of black rock sculpted by the elements, squatted atop the ridge to the southwest. To Dewey it looked like a giant Buddha contemplating the rice plain. Others had thought it resembled an ape, hence its name.

Shirtless, his upper torso showed tone earned from humping full rucksacks up and down the Central Highlands. Barely visible beneath his dark tan, a small, colorful skull with unfurled white wings and capped with an orange parachute grinned from his biceps. Below were blue letters that informed anyone interested enough to read them that he was indeed a paratrooper. Sweat, mixed with gritty dust, formed murky rivulets that pooled at the base of his spine, spreading in a dark stain over the seat of his pants.

The pungent aroma of burning hemp permeated the sticky air, thanks to a fuming pipe of marijuana passed among five young troopers gathered at the rear of the hooch. Yellow smoke drifted lazily over their heads as Green's radio blared from the rafters, filling the hooch with the gyrating music of Steppenwolf's *Don't Step on the Grass, Sam*. The small radio was tuned to Armed Forces Network, a group of stations that played music popular with teenagers both in Vietnam and back home in the Real World.

Green sat on a top bunk, his legs dangling over Iceman's impeccable afro, while Circus Boy sat, fat and nervous, on Frenchy's bunk. Frenchy lay on the plywood floor, head propped up on one elbow. Sand from the floor stuck to his sweat, creating a desert that covered his left side from hip to ribs. He reached with his free hand to accept a pipe trailing smoke and bursting seeds from Red, who barely had time to see it safely into Frenchy's hand before doubling up on the bunk next to Iceman, choking and gagging, smoke exiting his lungs in a fit of strangled coughs.

"I've told you and I've told you," Iceman said, reaching to accept the pipe from Frenchy. "But you just keep on bogartin'. Dig your dumb self, laying there dying because you get so damn greedy! When you going to learn moderation, my man? Moderation!" Tears streaming down his face, Red tried to talk but could not, and aimed a one-fingered salute at Iceman. "Now what is that supposed to be?" Iceman asked, holding the pipe like a perplexed professor. "Is it the amount of time you have left in Nam? Or possibly the number of white parents you have?"

Green let out a rebel yell, almost tumbling from his bunk as he leaned down to deliver a slap-five to Iceman's waiting palm. "Now I know why they call you the Iceman!" he laughed. "Yer cold, my man. Stone cold!"

"That's not it at all, Cracker. They call me The Iceman because I'm so cool."

Dewey smiled as he stared out over the rice plain at the sunset. He had come to know these men very well. He didn't understand them all of the time, but he knew them. Why Brown and Iceman got along at all was a mystery to him, one he did not probe. When the two got into their intellectual arguments over race, he gave them a wide berth.

Green would have been home months earlier had Top not nailed him for AWOL and pot, and gotten him six months in LBJ. He had not forgotten.

Iceman was a self-educated black trooper from the inner slums of Chicago; "Shy-Town," as he called it. He and Green were unlikely friends. Only Green could get away with calling Iceman a "nigger." Only Iceman could get away with slandering the South in Green's presence.

Dewey turned away from the sunset long enough to watch Circus Boy pass on the pipe, intent on rooting out a booger lodged at least two knuckles deep up in his cranium. Dewey smiled again and turned back to the sunset, thinking of Medlin, who had since gone back to The World. Circus Boy had Medlin to thank for his hated nickname. Circus Boy also knew his status with the group bordered on zero, though he did prove a useful gopher at times. He was considered a snitch, owing his allegiance to Top, kept in check only by his fear of the group.

Frenchy and Red were relatively quiet, rarely bucking the system openly. Both loved to get high on dew. Red took his nickname from the shock of orange hair he wore parted down the middle and the way his skin lobstered after just a few minutes in the Asian sun. He never tanned, just burned. Frenchy was actually Polish and just a touch slow. Not physically slow; on the contrary, he was one of the fastest runners Dewey had ever seen.

Months earlier, shortly after being airlifted off an obscure ridge in Ky Lo Valley, they had been surprised by MPs in Mama-San's East. Frenchy had sprinted between two tall MPs just as they'd reached the door, racing for the wire some three hundred meters away. The MPs had turned and given chase on foot. They really should not have bothered. Frenchy outdistanced them easily while Green and Dewey stole their jeep, embarking on a kamikaze run down the narrow highway to Tuy Hoa city.

A few miles down the crumbling stretch of road, they stopped to pick up two Air Force hitchhikers, abandoning them and the jeep in front of an off-limits bar. This after narrowly missing a chance to merge head-on with a convoy of trucks wearing signs warning of DANGER—HIGH EXPLOSIVES in three languages.

As he had passed the airmen to enter the bar, Dewey noted their ashen faces, shaking limbs, starched and pressed fatigues, spit-shined boots. One had pissed his pants.

Green and Dewey went straight through the back door of the Vietnamese bar and side-streeted until they found a quiet place where they kicked back with cold Cokes and drifted away on sweet-smelling smoke. Exchanging sideways glances, they laughed until their guts hurt before catching a ride on a Korean convoy back to the Herd's rear area.

Though the MPs began an intense investigation, Green, Frenchy, and Dewey were never charged. Dewey had returned to the field, first with Echo Raiders and then as Captain Wilson's RTO. He had paid his dues. He had earned a Purple Heart when an incoming RPG[15] had blown him off a bunker a month earlier, and had been credited with two confirmed kills. Now he thought of himself as an

---

15 Rocket-propelled grenade. A Soviet-designed anti-tank weapon also very useful against fortifications.

old-timer, a Sky Soldier, a bona fide member of the baddest bunch of fighting men in the world.

Staring at the sunset, he felt strong, young, lethal, and very deserving of the ten-thousand-piastre bounty the Viet Cong had placed on all their heads. Though the possibility of his death in combat had occurred to him, he could not yet conceive of an end to himself.

So he didn't believe in it.

He was thinking of Medlin again as he fingered the two shrunken bits of leather hanging from the thong around his neck.

"Yo! Dewey!" Green shouted, holding up a pipe giving off smoke like a Papal incense burner. "You want any of this?"

"Nah." Dewey answered absently, his eyes lingering on the sunset. Green instead passed it to Balisma, a lanky Louisianian who sometimes hung out with them.

A thin stroke of a memory surfaced in his thoughts and grew like a flowering vine as he turned to look down at Medlin's letter, recently arrived from The World. It lay open atop a jumble of gear he'd been packing into his ruck for tomorrow's return trip to the field. Dewey sat heavily on his cluttered bunk, sending springs creaking. The impact dislodged a stubby black cardboard cylinder about the size of a Drano can, which fell, rolled, and came to rest against Balisma's boot. The cylinder contained a canister with white letters printed on its side: GAS-CS.

For the twentieth time Dewey picked up Medlin's letter and scanned it, then decided to read it aloud. "Hey fellas…I heard from Medlin. Listen up. Here it is:

"Dear Dewey:

Well, I'm finally back in the World. Ya won't believe this but guys are wearing bell bottoms back here and there's a drug on the streets called LSD that's absolutely amazing!!!

By the way, somebody put a couple pounds of dew in the speakers I bought in Ahn Khe .... So they held my discharge up for two weeks but the Big Green Dick had to let me go! I'm a damn civilian!!!!! Speaking of big green dicks, I was told it was Top that tipped off the MPs. Somebody really oughta frag that bastard.

Hey! There's this song playing on the radio. It's amazingly mellow and seems to go on forever and ever. I fergit the name but it's off the new Beatles album. Yo, they just gave the name, it's "HEY JUDE," very nice.

Well, Dewey ol' boy, it this letter finds you in the field, good luck, Keep yer hed down and always remember, DBMH/2 . . . FTA. I love ya Bro.

Your Brother, MR. Medlin"

The men laughed as Dewey read the code letters that stood for "Don't Blow My High, Square," and "Fuck The Army." The same formulas were written in magic marker next to the black peace sign on his helmet's red-stained cloth camo cover. The ink monkeys had long since faded from rain and the jungle's constant dampness.

"Fuckin' Top," snarled Balisma. "That old bastard screws everyone. After that last Article 15 he's got me on long-term fuckin' berm guard duty."

"Ya think maybe he's VC?" said Green, taking a big hit on the pipe. "He fucked me over too."

"Worse," said Balisma, bending to pick up the black cardboard cylinder. Tossing it in one hand like an apple, he turned to face his friends. "Yo, Green! Ah thinks Ah gots me a Top Shelf idea."

Dewey would learn the precise specifics later, but it went down this way:

Balisma lay prone in the soft sand, awaiting Green and Frenchy to join him in the purple shadow of the mess tent. Fuck-you lizards cursed the darkness all around. Green flopped down next to Balisma in the sand, giggling almost hysterically.

"Where's Frenchy?" Balisma hissed, irritated.

"He don't want no part of this," gasped Green between giggle fits, tears squeezing from the corners of his eyes. "He's waiting with the others, over by the ammo bunker." He hooked a thumb over his shoulder, indicating a squat building a hundred yards away.

Balisma rose up on his elbows, barely able to make out darker shadows of men moving in the shadow of the ammo bunker. A match flared, illuminating a face; the flame flickered for a moment, then went out.

"Stupid assholes!" Balisma cursed under his breath. "Didn't you tell them to meet us at Mama-San's East?"

"Yeah, I did," Green answered, sobering a bit. "But what the hell? This promises to be one helluva shitshow. Besides, what harm can they do?"

"Shit! How ya gonna be, man? We could get nailed big time for this. Didja enjoy yer stay at LBJ?" Balisma hissed. "Think who's with 'em. That was Circus Boy's fat face Ah saw light up that smoke! And he's gonna watch us gas Top? How ya gonna be, Green?"

"He won't snitch, I'll personally see to that." Green smiled and threw a heavy arm across Balisma's shoulders. "Bro, ya crazy bastard, are we really gonna do this?"

"Betcha last peaches and pound cake on it!"

Returning Green's grin, Balisma rose quickly to his feet, crouching in the shadow. Holding his shoulder-slung weapon tightly against his left side and the tear gas canister in his right hand, he sprinted across twenty yards of open sand to the boardwalk of the Headquarters building. Flattening against the wall, he listened to his heart pounding. When he was certain he had not been seen, he motioned Green to follow.

An almost-full moon was rising above the mess tent, darkening the shadows and turning the sand luminescent silver. Top's room was around the north end of the building, adjacent to the supply sergeant's. Green flattened against the wall next to Balisma and they froze to listen for several seconds. Over Green's heavy breathing, Balisma could hear muffled voices drifting around the corner.

Balisma slid down the wall, keeping to the shadows, then peered with one eye around the corner. Top's door was slightly ajar. White light streamed out the crack in a bright slice. Without turning his head, Balisma motioned Green to follow as he slid around the corner.

The muffled voices grew louder, slightly slurred. Green bumped into Balisma as he stopped, just inches from Top's door; Balisma checked the hasp. The lock hung open from the door frame. Peering into the crack with one eye, he smiled, then eased back and turned to Green. "Jackpot. They're both in there."

Green leaned across Balisma to take a peek for himself. Top sat on the edge of his bunk in olive-drab boxer shorts under a dangling, bare 100-watt bulb. His skinny arms, face and neck were sunburned bright red but his upper torso and legs were milk-white and bony. A tuft of grey hair met the red V left on his chest by wearing his shirt open at the collar. His face was crinkled into a perpetual frown. Obviously drunk, he was cursing loudly, blowing spittle into the obese face of the supply sergeant who straddled a metal chair drawn up to Top's bedside. The supply sergeant was nodding in the affirmative while tilting a waning bottle of Jack Daniels to his lips.

Green eased the lock from the hasp, nodding to Balisma while reaching to coax the door open a little wider.

Top was busy telling the supply sergeant just what he'd like to do to all the low-life potheads in the brigade as Balisma pulled the pin on the canister. Green's eyes met his and he hesitated, savoring the moment. Then, with a slight flick of the wrist, he tossed the canister toward the light bulb. He caught a quick glimpse of Top's face as the canister detonated in mid-air with a loud *POP!* Top's eyes followed the canister as it fell to the floor, his mouth wide open. Balisma slammed the door shut and pressed the hasps together as Green quickly slapped the lock home and snapped it shut.

They turned and ran toward the ammo bunker, the hiss of tear gas suddenly overwhelmed by shouts of anger and disbelief from behind Top's locked door. As they passed the bunker, the group waiting there joined them. Only when they were well down the road to La Bah did they turn to watch the drama unfold.

Clouds of white gas poured like smoke from the screen above Top's door. The door shattered as Top burst through it like a skinny quarterback plowing his way into the end zone, closely followed by the waddling hulk of the supply sergeant. Both men were coughing and gagging as they stumbled away from the billowing cloud of gas. Something brown barber-poled down Top's legs as he collapsed to his knees in the sand, vomiting.

The group stood in absolute silence, watching the results of Balisma's dirty deed. Far back, across moonscape dunes, a white pall poured out of the NCO's quarters and drifted over tiny figures scurrying like ants around a freshly kicked anthill.

"That's for the six months you wasted of my life, you bastard!" Green snarled. Turning to the others, he chortled: "The sonuvabitch shit hisself. Didja see that? He shit hisself!"

Laughter swept the group as they danced a victory jig together. All except one.

"That wasn't such a good idea," Circus Boy whined. "Tear gas is dangerous. They might have been hurt bad. The shit's gonna hit the fan over this for sure. You guys went too far this time."

The laughter and dancing stopped as if on cue. It grew suddenly very quiet. For a moment, no one moved.

"Fuck hurt!" Green exclaimed, jabbing a stiff finger into Circus Boy's pudgy chest. "And fuck far! That sonuvabitch has done us all dirty! You included, ya fuckin' leg[16]! But yer too much of an ass-kisser to give a shit 'bout that! Ain'tcha, Circus Boy! Ain'tcha?"

With each word Green poked harder, pushing him back a step with each jab. Circus Boy's mouth worked silently like he was trying to speak. He looked down at his boots, pushing his glasses back up his nose.

Balisma stepped between the two. He shoved his face into Circus Boy's until their noses touched. He drawled in a tone he might have used to invite a friend to go fishing. "Open yer mouth to anyone, anyone, and yer dead meat. Ah'll cut yer friggin' throat. Understand, faggot?"

Circus Boy's blood chilled. He knew Balisma meant what he said.

"I didn't say I'd tell," he sputtered, holding his arms out in an exaggerated shrug while looking from face to face for support. "I just think it was a bad idea."

He didn't see Frenchy sneak up behind him on all fours. Balisma's eyes burned into Circus Boy's until Frenchy was sideways behind his legs. Then Balisma shoved violently, pushing Circus Boy backward over Frenchy, causing Circus Boy to land hard on his

---

16 Airborne-qualified U.S. Army soldiers have long referred to those not jump-qualified as "legs," usually prefixed as Green did here. Directed at another jumper, it could be taken as deeply insulting depending on the tone—especially in this context.

back. Wind knocked out, he lay gasping for air on the moonlit sand as Balisma turned on his heel and strode toward the village. "Fuck that jerk," he said to no one in particular. "Let's go get laid."

Minus Circus Boy, the group fell in behind Green. Some started laughing again but the laughter had lost most of its mirth. Dewey looked back at Circus Boy, who had risen to one knee and was hugging his chest.

I remember another kid, not long ago, who desperately wanted to belong.

Dewey felt a twinge of shame and a sudden surge of sympathy for the fat kid, but didn't let his thoughts show as he hurried to catch up with the group.

They'd traveled a hundred yards or so when Circus Boy shouted angrily behind them. "You bastards! I'm gonna—"

Green whipped around, aimed his M-16, and fired one tracer round just inches over Circus Boy's head. For the second time that night Circus Boy found himself hitting the sand hard, this time face down. A red laser beam streaked out over the berm, winking on and off under the stars until it was gone. A split second later, Circus Boy was on his feet running as fast as a fat man can run in loose sand, back to the safety of the rear area.

Green turned and resumed his trek toward La Bah. The others stood motionless watching Circus Boy run, bawling like a dog kicked down a dirty alley.

"Think he'll tell?" Frenchy asked quietly.

"Would you?" Dewey asked, lost in thought, turning to follow Green and Balisma.

They could hear the South China Sea long before they saw it: a gentle hushing of breakers rolling endlessly onto the beach. Soft lamp lights floated in windows of La Bah where the fishing village sprawled amid moon-shadows of palms and litchis. As they turned toward the waiting bunker, Dewey could see the waves, their crests faintly glowing with green phosphorescence. He felt a twinge of déjà vu as he flopped onto the rotting sandbags. It seemed like last night he'd gotten high here for the first time.

Looking out to where the Milky Way met the sea, he felt a tide of acute homesickness burn inside with an ache that ebbed out onto a beach of pure pride. For all that he had been through, saw through, knew he still had to go through, he was proud to be part of this war. Home would be nice for a night or two, and he was slated to return home in six months anyhow. He wondered what the hippies were doing. God, how he hated them, Jane Fonda especially. He turned back to his friends, tuning in to an escalating verbal bout between Iceman and Green.

"What're you looking at, you silly-faced, racist cracker? All I said was that the white race is doomed. Allah is coming down, real soon, to straighten all this honky shit out. The white crackers will be burned by his breath to crispy critters."

"Eat shit and die, nigger," Green retorted. "I told you what we gonna do with them there canisters of sickle-cell anemia virus after I get my young ass back to The World. Shee-it. Just think of it. Every lake, river 'n stream. Gawd, what a plan! No more welfare, no mo' crime and best of all, no more niggers!"

"Listen, you red-necked pig-fucking cracker, I got half a mind to slap you up 'long-side your head. Wouldn't do no good though. If you had a brain, it'd just rattle around inside you skull like a bee-bee in a box car." Iceman sat solemnly, folding his arms in mock indignation. Then he shot a smiling, sideways glance at Green. "Damn racist cracker!"

Green leapt at The Iceman and they clinched atop the bunker like a couple of fighting cocks. The others moved out of their way as they wrestled and rolled around calling each other "nigger" or "cracker."

This was nothing new. No one interfered.

Moments later they ceased their play, joining the others crouching lower in the sand behind the bunker. The approaching whine of a jeep engine grew louder. Headlights briefly illuminated their hiding place as the MPs left the village, turning down a sandy road that followed the perimeter of the wire. They stayed hidden, watching the jeep fade until it was only a flicker of ruby taillights bouncing far down the road.

Green stood and strode toward the break in the wire, the others following. Guards in the nearest tower greeted them with hoots and lewd jokes that the troopers flung back, laughing as they picked their way through coils of razor wire.

Dewey was thinking about how good an ice-cold Coke would taste and how this would be the last time he would get laid for quite a while when he heard Tiger's high-pitched voice calling his name. "Boot! Hey, Boot!"

He had no problem picking Tiger out of the milling crowd of street urchins waiting on the village side of the wire. As the first soldiers crossed over, the kids descended upon them like minnows on a piece of bread, tugging at their uniforms and chattering in pidgin English. Green scattered them with a verbal burst of agitated Vietnamese.

The kids knew these were no suckers. The main crowd of children backed off, muttering their disappointment but willing to wait for less experienced prey. Dewey had long since learned that street kids were a mixed blessing. They were an excellent barometer for determining the status of the village. If kids were around, it was safe to enter. If there were no kids—or they melted away in great haste—

then either MPs or VC were in the village, or there was some other dangerous situation.

They were also the world's most adept pickpockets. Their ability to slit a GI's wallet pocket with a razor blade was legendary. Most FNGs, being young and for the most part kindly souls, pitied the ragged kids. That made them easy pickings. While a swarm of street urchins kept an FNG busy guarding his front, another kid would slit his back pocket and fade away with the FNG's wallet, followed shortly by his accomplices. The children were able to pull that trick only once per trooper as most GIs learned it with one lesson, but there were a few exceptionally slow Americans. Dewey knew one who'd lost his wallet twice—along with two gold watches.

Tiger had gotten him.

As the street kids closed on Dewey in the moonlight, he saw many wearing clothes his parents had sent in packages, per his request months earlier. "Baby-sans, *di-di maow*![17]" he shouted with authority. All the kids scattered but one.

Tiger sauntered up to Dewey on bare feet mottled with dust, hands tucked deep into his pockets and an ear-to-ear smile under the saddest Madras hat in the world. He wore lime-green pants with the cuffs rolled up, and a tattered once-white shirt haphazardly tucked into his waistband. A combination of Asian Dondi and Forty-Second Street pimp, Tiger was a scrapper who effectively controlled his band of thieves despite being half the size of most. Dewey admired his spunk. Tiger had a lot of that, but he didn't have a left eye. What he had was a glistening grey orb surrounded by lumpy, violet scar tissue.

"Yo, Green! I'll meetcha at Mama-San's!" Dewey shouted after his buddies as they faded under the banyan trees.

---

17 "Get out of here!" An expression that survived in Army slang for decades following Vietnam.

Green waved his acknowledgment as he vanished into the shadows. Dewey dropped to one knee in the sand and rumpled Tiger's straight black hair. Tiger flinched away and lost his smile for a moment, then reached out and rubbed his small brown hand through Dewey's curly locks.

"Hey Boot!" he called. "I thought you fini here! I think you go already back field! Maybe you no go back field? Maybe you stay in La Bah a long time? Yes, Boot?"

"I fini here, for sure," Dewey answered, exchanging palm slaps with Tiger. "I go back field tomorrow. Tonight, I party good! Here," he added, reaching into the deep utility pockets of his jungle fatigues. "These are for you."

Tiger's smile widened along with his good eye as Dewey filled his skinny arms with sealed canvas pouches about the size of books. They were in various compositions: beef and rice, chicken and rice, chili, spaghetti and meatballs, etc.

"Numbah fahking one, Boot!" Tiger exclaimed over his growing load, his good eye shimmering big and brown, the ruined one glinting dully in the moonlight."Mama-San like beaucoup! Sop sop numbah one! Maybe next time you bring much Salems? Yes?"

"Next time? You little con, Tiger, my main man, yer somethin' else!" Dewey shook Tiger's thin shoulders, careful not to spill the lurps from their precarious perch. "Next time gonna be a loooooooooong time, Tiger." Pulling his wallet out, he looked Tiger in the eye. "There is somethin' ya kin do fer me tonight. Tell ya what I need. *Ihng chaw toy cahn sai. Ihng biet, cahn sai? Ihng hue toy?*"

"*Toy biet*! You beaucoup yak-yak Vietnam now, Boot! Same, same Green. But he yak-yak more beaucoup! How much cahn sai, Boot?"

"Lookey here," Dewey said, hoisting his slipping M-16 strap back upon his shoulder. "You get me this much cahn sai." Using his index fingers he drew a shape in the air about the size of a small loaf of bread. Then he took an orange and white military payment certificate from his wallet and tucked the Monopoly-type, five-dollar bill into Tiger's shirt pocket.

"Cum sow! I get! But you give too much MPC, Boot!"

"I know how much I gave ya, Tiger. No sweat, I souvenir you the change. Now," he added in a stern voice, indicating the lurps threatening to spill from Tiger's arms, "get that shit home! I'll be layin' up with Chai Co at Mama-San's East. Meet me there. Okay? Good. Now, di di maow!"

"Hokay, Boot!" Tiger sang out as he tottered over the crushed seashell sand.

Dewey watched the boy disappear into shadows with his shifting load of lurps, remembering how different cultural voice patterns had changed both their names.

Tiger's real name, if it was his real name, sounded very much like 'tigah.' While Dewey suspected that the kid had assumed a macho alias, he didn't care. Tiger was Tiger, a war-wise kid who couldn't pronounce 'Dewey.' Tiger couldn't pronounce 'Vince' either. After a long, fruitless session of trying to teach the kid to say 'Dewey' correctly, he'd tried the nickname his parents had tagged him with. "Okay, Tiger, try this. Watch my lips. Butch. *Ihng biet*? Butch!"

"Hokay!" Tiger laughed. "You Boot!"

"No. No. No. My name is Butch! See. Buu..ttt..chhh. Now, try it again."

Tiger laughed then steeled his features into a mask of comic concentration, spitting out "Boot!"

"Noooo! BUTCH! Can't you understand English? Butch! Try it again."

"I say that already! Boot! Boot! Boot! Boot!" Tiger shot back, his good eye glistening with anger.

"Hokay." Dewey sighed. "You call me Boot."

Mama-San's East was a ramshackle conglomeration of wood, cardboard, and corrugated tin. Its sole purpose was to cater to the sexual needs of Americans and sometimes the Koreans stationed nearby. The house of ill repute was tolerated by the fishing village only for the vast sums of dollars that flowed from it into the pockets and coffers of the village chief.

The building was set back beyond more respectable houses, surrounded by banyan trees and scruffy, withered bushes holding a precarious grip on life. A raised wooden porch covered the front of the one-story building whose corrugated tin roof gleamed in moonlight above shadowy figures where Dewey's friends had gathered around the rough-hewn wood railing and stairs.

Their voices floated to him with brittle clarity. Exchanging cutting quips with Frenchy, they jostled around his whore, grab-assing, titty-squeezing, and making lewd, detailed suggestions. Frenchy's whore leaned over the railing, laughing and sing-songing phrases in tittering Vietnamese to other whores filling two large windows that over looked the porch. She wore a see-through wisp of a pale lavender shirt over black silk pajama pants. As Dewey drew closer, he could see her true appeal silhouetted by the moonlight.

Breasts. Large, full, firm, ripe breasts. Honest to God, back on the farm, healthy mammary glands that were so very rare in Vietnam. So rare that Frenchy's whore had the only adult, Western-sized breasts in the whole village of La Bah, hence her immediate popularity.

When she saw Dewey approaching, she squeezed her breasts together with her arms and leaned forward, further accenting her cleavage. He felt a stirring desire in his groin as his eyes slipped over the gentle, peach-fuzzed roundness. His desire shriveled as he drew close enough to catch a strong whiff of her. The woman gave off an overpowering stench, sort of a mixture between stale sweat and dead fish.

And her breath could melt down a small truck.

She had a round, ruined face with all the appeal of an abused potato too long held in the bin.

Frenchy had professed to love her. He had even gone so far as to petition the brass for permission to marry her and take her back to The World. Top had flushed the paperwork, citing her profession and Frenchy's age as deterrents, adding her medical rap sheet as a clincher. She still operated as a whore, but never when Frenchy came to town. The two intended to be married by a Buddhist monk before Frenchy's tour ended. Dewey didn't think either one of them were serious about the love angle of their relationship. He figured Frenchy to be using her for a free lay and that she planned to dump Frenchy as soon as she got into the States.

As Dewey mounted the steps, Frenchy was descending with his whore, still fending off the advances of Red, Green, and Iceman. As they passed, while Frenchy had his head turned to bark at Green, his whore reached out and cupped Dewey's genitals with a gentle squeeze. Dewey smiled and rolled his eyes as he followed the others into Mama-San's East. Frenchy and his whore slipped into the shadows under the banyan trees, arm in arm, heading for the beaches of the South China Sea.

Chai Co cut him off, sidling up to the doorjamb with exaggerated coyness. She wore a white shift with a Nehru collar, slit almost to her waist on both sides. A tanned, well-defined thigh peeked out as she tossed her long hair into a brief ebony fan.

"Soooo, Baby-san want Mama-san?" she crooned, framed by yellow lamplight as her thick, black, shining hair settled over her shoulders. Then she stood very straight and placed both hands on her hips, continuing in a mocking voice. "No way, GI! You too young! You baby-san! How you know make boom-boom? How you know do love? You maybe numbah ten kid for sure! Yes?"

"Yes!" Dewey shouted, scooping her waist and dragging her tight to his chest. "I numbah fuckeeng ten baby-san all right! All I want to do is fuck! Fuck all day!"

He drew her face close, until their eyelashes touched, then continued as he pretended to twist a mustache he couldn't grow yet. "Fuck all night! Whattaya say, wench? You numbah fuckeeng ten too, kid?"

Green lounged just inside the door, sitting in a bamboo recliner under a drifting haze of sweet-smelling incense with a can of Coca-Cola. He rattled something off in Vietnamese so fast and fluent Dewey was unable to catch a word of it. Laughing, Chai Co collapsed into Dewey's arms, then twisted around to chortle a similar burst back at Green just as he had a mouthful of soda. He laughed, choking and spewing Coke across the sandy clapboard floor.

"Uh-uh, none of that shit," Dewey cautioned, drawing Chai Co into the room by her hand. Little streams of incense smoke followed, curly-cuing in their wake. He led her to another bamboo recliner just across the table from Green.

"What were you two talking about?" he asked her, sitting heavily, drawing her down onto his lap.

"Him say not to worry. You dick too small make boom-boom! He say you dick same-same monkey baby-san!"

Dewey lunged to steady a glass oil lamp his heavy sit-down had jostled. The table had once held cabling for the Navy and was covered by white silk salvaged from parachute flares sewn together into a rather slippery tablecloth. Incense drifted in sweet clouds from a cast bronze statue of Buddha who hunched near the lamp, fat and sassy, contemplating the glowing ember in the bowl at his feet.

Dewey could hear Green chuckling into his soda can as he opened the hollow handle of his hunting knife and poured marijuana from it to fill a pipe. "So what'd ya say back to him?" he asked Chai Co as he packed his bowl.

"I say, not to worry. Dewey still puppy. Him balls no drop yet! No sweat for me!" Chai Co slipped down to his feet and busied herself with his laces, already in the process of slipping off one boot.

"I'm a puppy, huh?" he said, passing the pipe over her back to a silently grinning Iceman. "That means you must be a pussy."

"Poosey?" Chai Co exclaimed, leaping to her feet, seemingly aghast. She arched one thin black eyebrow and placed her left hand on a jutted hip as she leaned forward to point into her nonexistent cleavage. "I numbah one Cherry Girl! Go to church school! Papa-san 'portant zecutive in govament! I beaucoup Virgin Mary, mothafucka! You be nice to me or Papa-san, he shoot you dead!"

She held her eyebrow raised for a moment, then broke out in a chortling burst of laughter as she turned, wiggled her ass in Dewey's face, and skipped over to the ice chest to get him a soda. "You better be careful." Green said, still chuckling as a fresh-faced Vietnamese girl lit his pipe with a long match. "She's a firefight all by herself."

Suddenly the night sky beyond the window filled with silent streams of red tracers pouring from the Korean encampment beyond the Herd's rear area. They cut the night like red laser beam pick-up-sticks spilled abruptly over black velvet. The clouds Dewey had watched crawling over the mountains earlier had finally closed off the stars. Heavier rounds, fifty-calibers, winked on and off all the way across the paddies to ricochet off the mountains. The smaller-caliber tracers made it only halfway across before burning out like thousands of red fireflies.

Dewey and the others stared at the light show for several seconds as after-images left by spent tracers turned green on their retinas, crisscrossing current red tracers. The metallic grinding of scores of heavy machine guns firing simultaneously reached the hooch and continued for several minutes before tapering off ten seconds after the last few tracers winked out. "I wonder how much money they waste every night with that shit," Red murmured, downing his Coke in a series of ice-cold swallows and banging the can down hard.

"Just so's they can swagger over those rice paddies with fire. All bought and paid for with American taxpayer loot."

"Yeah, that's true," Iceman answered, still mesmerized by laser like after-images of tracers. "They some bad dudes, them ROKs. I just be glad they on our side. Let 'em swagger."

"Sure," Green laughed, hoisting the smoldering pipe and gesturing back toward the Herd's berm. "They bad, but ask Dewey about the chicken battle he fought with Balisma while they was on Berm guard yesterday."

"It was one heck of a shootin' match!" Dewey interjected, before the faces turning to him could ask. "Balisma scared the crap outta me!

"We wuz atop the bunker, sipping hot cocoa and gettin' toked up just as the sun was rising. Well, there was these colorful chickens scratching and digging in the dirt around that little village just beyond the berm. Balisma just up and said, 'watch this' and hauled off and popped a cap on one of those chickens, and hey! The bird just exploded! No, really! It exploded in a big puff of orange feathers.

"So I said, "Hey, I'll get that one with the red and black feathers." These chickens were about a hundred yards away, no shit! We spent the next half hour wastin' all of 'em. Musta exploded about thirty of 'em! Then, long about the time we run out of chickens; they was all lyin' in pools of feathers'n shit, when out come this man from the village. He just sauntered out into the shit field, dropped his drawers, squatted, and shit. Just like that. He was starin' off at the mountains and shittin' so peaceful like with the sun breaking the horizon.

"So's I said to Balisma, 'Ten bucks on the shittin' man,' and I lay down on the sandbags in the prone position. Balisma, he was goin' nuts, sayin', 'Don't be shootin' that man!,' and shit like that. Well, I put that black bead right at his feet and squeezed reeaall slow. Crack!

"The round hit no more than six inches in front of his toes, sent up a big whuff of dust too! The guy fell over backwards and jumped up running! His pants were still down around his ankles and he kept falling down! He was shakin' his fist at us and runnin' and cussin' in Vietnamese all the way into the ville! Must have fell down ten, twenty times but was too scared to stop and hoist his britches!"

The four young troopers laughed, smoked their pipes, and fondled their whores. This was Dewey's going-away party of sorts, and they sat recalling the tear-gassing of Top, along with every other crazy episode they'd shared in the past few months, until around midnight when the old Vietnamese woman who ran the whorehouse waltzed into the room. "Hey boys! You do fine tonight? Come see Mama-San? Yes?"

She smiled out from an incredibly wrinkled face. Her eyes sparkled with life, two brown beads shimmering among thousands of tiny crow's feet. She couldn't have weighed more than seventy pounds and her back was bent by the years into a near-hunchbacked stoop, under a tight bun of grey hair that hung to the nape of her neck.

Green jumped up and took her hand, speaking animated Vietnamese as he led her back to his chair. The girl who had been filling his pipe and stroking his chest folded her arms as she stood to make room for her boss. She shot a peevish glance across the room to Chai Co, who sent a casual shrug back.

Mama-San loved Green like a son. She had been his benefactor during the six months he had spent AWOL in-country. She had taught him most of the Vietnamese he knew. Now she doted on him whenever he came by and they would sometimes sit for hours conversing in Vietnamese punctuated by laughter.

"So, Dew man, why you wanna mess with the field?" Iceman asked, obviously more interested in the squirmy little whore on his lap, giggling with one hand stuck down his pants. He looked over at Dewey as he extracted her hand and set her back away from him on the sofa."You don't need that shit, man. Ain't a firebase bad enough for ya? They got mortared again last night, ya know, and they got this sniper that pops a full mag at 'em three times a day. From a different firing point each time. Ain't that bad enough for ya, Dewd? Whatcha wanna do, die? You a crazy mothafucka, Dewey. Volunteering' like that. Sheeit! Didn't anyone ever tell you, never volunteer for nothin'?"

"Whoah, how ya gonna be, Iceman? It ain't like I never done this before, ya know."

"You know what I mean. You could be sittin' up top some relay station, playing Aussie coast watcher or some such shit. Remember when you lost over three hundred dollars playing acey-deucy with Fyle? We was up there for weeks, just you, me, Frenchy, and those squads from Alpha Company. Tell me that wasn't boonie enough for ya."

"Of course I remember! I made those cards out of C-rat meal boxes! And I still owe Fyle beaucoup bucks. How could I forget?" Dewey answered, irritated. "Now I got a question for you! How many times you have been shot at, been mortared and rocketed? How many?" He went on before Iceman could answer. "Many! And how many times you been able to shoot back? Very fuckin' seldom! At least I get that chance out there. If I fuck up, then *sin loy*! It was my fuckup. But you just be walkin' across the firebase, enjoyin' the hot sun and thinkin' bout yer bitch back in The World and *pow*, yer dead. Sheeit! A mortar round could take our asses out right here, right now…any damn time.

"Besides," Dewey paused to puff the pipe back to life with loud popping sounds, "I can't deal with all the Mickey Mouse shit that goes on back here or even out on the firebase. Yeah, I'm talkin' Top and all the other fuckin' lifers. Now I'm responsible to Captain Wilson again, and myself. But on the real side and to close my case, I'm the best. I can smell an ambush and I move down them trails like a ghost. Ain't but one guy in the company got as many confirmed kills as me. I'm a born hunter. The boonies? Hell yeah! They suit me fine."

"Yeah, well, I still think yer crazy. But that's for you to live, not me."

"That's right." Dewey snapped.

"No, I think yer wrong," Iceman intoned, his voice trailing off as he melted into the sofa with his whore. "Hey, Green!" he shouted. "I see you've finally found a woman you can handle!"

"Fuck off and die, nigger!" Green chuckled. "Mama-San would break your black back!"

Iceman started to say something but Tiger's arrival interrupted him. He burst into the room and slammed the door shut behind him, then whirled around to face them, his back against the door, hair mussed and gasping for breath. His good eye opened as wide as his ruined one as he sat down in an exhausted heap at Dewey's feet. "Fahk! Korean GI numbah fahkeeng ten!" Tiger stopped to gasp for air. "Korean GI beaucoup dinky-dow! Fahking drunk! Try to cockadile me!" He sat up and drew a stubby finger across his throat. "But I run like jeep!"

Tiger's breathing was becoming more regular as he talked, and his good eye sparkled over a crooked grin. "They too drunk. Fall down in shit field! On face! Here Boot, catch!" He tossed a crumpled brown paper bag up to Dewey. "Is good, yes?"

Dewey caught the bag with one hand and hefted it, feeling its weight, then stuck his nose into the bag and breathed. It smelled omnipotent, very aromatic in a rich, musty sort of way. "Is good." He nodded down to Tiger, giving the thumbs-up. "Is very good."

Later, after Green had been led away from Mama-San by the giggling young whore, with Green describing in Vietnamese exactly what he was going to do to her, Tiger went back out into the night. Chai Co turned to Dewey, her brown eyes liquid soft.

"You want take shower?" She uncoiled from his lap with a shy smile, tugging gently on his hand until he rose with her. She led him down dark corridors into the back of the whorehouse, the oil lamp in her hand spilling knee-deep shadows from its flickering flame.

The shower was behind the ramshackle house. It consisted of a sun-warmed, rusty fifty-gallon drum supported by a plank platform on two-by-fours just over head-high. A rotted rope connected to a valve lever controlled the sprinkler. There was no curtain.

Behind the little shower, twenty yards beyond the last of the banyan trees, was the shit field. It was littered with small, wadded pieces of paper whose source and purpose were obvious. Dewey smiled at the memory from a few months earlier, when the big brass had called all the line troops in out of the field and closed off the bases. No civilians were allowed on, nor soldiers allowed off. No one knew what was happening and the rumor mill thrived about major battles brewing—perhaps even an end to the war. It turned out that the controlling forces had attempted to cripple the black market by changing the Military Payment Certificates the US troops used as currency. They invalidated all the current funny money, then reissued a whole new series of bills with changed color schemes and designs. After the change was completed, they allowed the troopers to take advantage of the stand-down by giving out passes.

Of course, not everyone had been in full compliance. Dewey had gone into Tuy Hoa city without waiting for a pass. Arriving several hours before any other GIs, he found the black market in howling disarray. Old women followed him down crowded side streets, begging him to exchange their worthless MPC for them. They offered up to eighty percent of their stuffed pillowcases and shoe boxes full of worthless currency as an incentive.

At first he tried to ignore them, but, after several blocks of being trailed by wailing black marketers, he whirled on one. Grabbing a fistful of bills out of her shoebox, he drew it over the crack of his ass in a wiping motion, tossing the worthless paper in the air. "This number ten!" he scolded. "You on yer own, Mama-San! Sin loy, del Mammy!"

A few nights later, while relieving himself behind Mama-San's East, he'd noticed crumpled and stained old MPC bills of various denominations scattered over the shit field. He laughed himself to tears when he saw how their status had been so drastically altered and had given a whole new meaning to the term "dirty money."

The clouds were breaking up again, thinning and thickening, turning the moon on and off. From a small distance, he watched Chai Co lay out towels, her white shift fading in and out of lamplight that flickered more strongly when the moon went out.

He was thinking about how there was so much that he didn't know about this pretty Vietnamese girl. He also knew he really didn't care. Her past meant less to him than what he would eat for breakfast in the morning. But at times like this, when she was wrapped in her Asian mystique and making sure everything was just right before they made love, he did wonder, and did care.

He'd asked her once how any creature as lovely as she had come to peddle her ass in a makeshift tin and cardboard hut. And where her family was, and why she was fucking any GI who came up with five hundred piaster's, a camouflaged poncho liner, or a carton of Salems. Chai Co had become very agitated. "Mama-San, Papa-San, they die! House, he fini too! Girl got to eat. Goddam! I never charge you, Doo-ay! What a girl 'posed to do?"

He never asked again.

The moon emerged from behind the clouds as Chai Co let her shift slip from her shoulders. It pooled, milk-white, about her ankles. As she stepped daintily from the puddle of her dress, Dewey felt his heartbeat grow deeper.

Together, we're like the moon, he thought, his eyes caressing her firm, peach-sized breast. *She's almost full and my head's in the clouds.*

The water had lost whatever heat it had borrowed from the day and they gasped in unison as cold water hit them. Dewey was soaping Chai Co with a large, sea-caught sponge as the moon came out again. He watched her face slide slowly down his chest, her small pink tongue flickering over his nipples, lingering in his navel, until she knelt in front of him, her wet black hair shining in moonlight. One cool hand gently cupped his testicles and the other rested like a thin, brown moth on his white buttocks. He leaned his head back, silently barking at the moon as her mouth became a soft, warm wetness made all the more pleasurable by the barely perceptible threat of pearly white teeth slipping up and down his erection.

Somewhere in the darkness, not far beyond Mama-San's East, a short burst of M-16 fire preceded the loud *whoumph* of an explosion. Dewey instantly dropped to the shower's gravel floor, taking Chai Co down hard with him as his orgasm doubled him over and he came in violent spurts. For several long minutes they lay there, breathing heavily, waiting for other explosions that didn't come.

Diced by mosquito screens, sunlight poured through the bunkhouse as Dewey entered, allowing the spring-loaded screen door to bang shut behind him. He looked rumpled and very tired.

Circus Boy, his hair still glistening from a recent shower, sat on his bunk putting a last brushing on the toes of his spit-shined Corcoran boots. He looked up, squinting into the sunlight as Dewey dropped onto his own bunk with a mad creak of springs.

"Lotsa shit in the air this morning!" Circus Boy called out cheerfully, his voice dripping with innuendo. "Top's called a real damn formation. Yep, lotta shit in the air!" He paused, looking over at Dewey, his eyes narrowing. "Top and the supply sergeant spent the night in the medic's tent, ya know. You guys really messed him up. He could've died, ya know."

"Eat shit and die, lifer," Dewey said as he locked his hands behind his head and stared up at Green's radio, still stuck in the rafters' crotch. *I Heard It Through the Grapevine*, a song very popular at the time with teenagers both back in The World and in South Vietnam, thumped electronically in the background. "You open your mouth to anyone and I'll cut yer fat-assed heart out and feed it to you. *Ihng biet*, faggot?"

He stuck his hand out and pulsed his fingers as if they held a living, beating heart.

"No, I wouldn't tell! You don't have to worry about me, Dewey," Circus Boy answered quickly, licking his lips. "I've only got to do another month here. I ain't a-lookin' for no hassles. There's more to this formation than just Top's gettin' gassed. Some drunken Korean tried to climb the berm wire last night, right by the path through to La Bah. The guards in the tower said some street kid led him there, shouting nasty things about the Korean's mother. Well, the tower guards yelled somethin' at the Korean that pissed him off enough to climb the goddam wire and go after 'em. They tried to warn him about the minefield. Even shot a burst into the ground in front of him. He was too drunk and set on kicking their asses to understand. Still, he got halfway through the minefield before he found one. Blew his foot clean off. They had a helluva time getting him out of there. Had to bring in a chopper. Top's got what's left of his boot nailed to the wall, just outside the CQ door..."

Circus Boy winced and his voice trailed off as he noticed Dewey wasn't paying attention. He brushed at his boots one more time and stood, looking down at Dewey stretched out on his bunk. "Well, I gotta run, I'm on CQ duty," Circus Boy said as he tucked a starched fatigue shirt crackling into his pants. "What time's yer chopper taking off?"

"Zero nine thirty." Dewey answered, not bothering to open his eyes. "Make sure you send a runner to wake me up at 0900."

Circus Boy looked down at Dewey with disgust, shaking his head from side to side. "Top really could've died last night, ya know."

"Tell it to someone who cares, asswipe." Dewey murmured.

"Well, anyway, keep yer head down out there," Circus Boy said with a shrug as he turned to the door. "I'll pray for God to look out fer ya."

"I wouldn't worry about it," Dewey murmured again as the door banged shut behind Circus Boy. "Paratroopers are gods."

November 1st, 1968

Over the Central Highlands, Republic of Vietnam (resumed)

The supply chopper was suddenly jolted by turbulence, shaking Dewey awake with a start. Out the open door, far below, rice paddies still blazed briefly with sun as it set each paddy afire just before the tiny shadow of their UH-1 reached them. The old man he had watched run from his water buffalo just a few minutes earlier was gone now, but the big Indian seemed not to have moved; he was still staring back toward the South China Sea, wearing the same blank expression he had worn since the MPs had forced him onto the aircraft at gunpoint.

Dewey mentally shrugged as he leaned over to look out his own door. He watched as the chopper's shadow flashed over the last paddy dike and collided with the wall of mountains marking the beginning of the Central Highlands. Dewey's brief nap had energized him somewhat from the hangover of his going-away party the night before in La Bah. The chopper's black shadow flickered up the near-vertical slope, wriggling and leaping over ebony rocks and green brush like a giant black salmon leaping up a waterfall. Abruptly the shadow crossed the ridge, where it rippled over treetops hiding the jungle floor for as far as he could see.

The treetops look like tiny cauliflowers.

Both door gunners test-fired their weapons as they crossed the invisible line of demarcation into the free kill zone—Indian country, they called it. Anyone in the highlands below not allied with the U.S. was considered the enemy. The casings of the door gunners' M-60s fell away in lines like tiny, gleaming brass bombs.

Grinning, he leaned further out into the rotor wash. The Central Highlands seemed to go forever. A lush carpet of foliage, dotted with circular, water-filled bomb craters of various sizes, covered the hills and valleys below as far as the human eye could see.

A few minutes later, looking out far ahead of the chopper's rippling shadow, he could just make out a small scar on the flat of a distant plateau. He watched the jagged scar grow for ten minutes, putting his helmet on only after the craft turned to circle in.

He hated coming in low over the jungle this way, be it a combat assault or a milk run return to the forward FSB, such as this mission. As the chopper skimmed the treetops, he leaned far back into the craft. His face felt like a target. He had a fear, one he kept to himself, of an incoming bullet seeking his face every time he sat in the open door of a Huey…like now. He felt extremely vulnerable, even after they flew over the rolls of razor wire, trenches, and fields of burnt-off vegetation encircling the small, isolated base. Red-stained fighting bunkers squatted on each point and crotch of the zigzagging perimeter. He never got used to it. It all seemed so surreal.

Boonie rats, as any forward troops were called, scrambled all over the small base trying to escape the Huey's rotor wash and resulting storm of wind-driven debris as the chopper followed the billow of purple smoke pluming over the heart of the firebase.

A large olive-drab canvas medic's tent swelled next to the circus-sized mess tent. The firebase crawled with dust-stained boonie rats amid clusters of olive-drab poncho hooches, some of which had fatigues hanging off support ropes. He watched in amusement as the hooches and fatigues were blown helter-skelter despite their owners' best efforts to rescue them.

Tall, thick elephant grass tossed frantically then flattened, shaking violently as if bowing to some heathen god as the resupply chopper settled onto the LZ one skid at a time. Dewey didn't wait until the craft ceased movement. He shouldered his heavy rucksack, balanced his weapon on his right hip's ammo pouch, then climbed down onto a skid and dropped into the grass. He slipped away from the craft in a low crouch as the whirling blades sucked veils of purple smoke up, then over and into the main blades where it dissipated in the hurricane breath of the hovering metal bird.

Ingland met him alongside a mountain of pallets stacked high with C-rations and slightly larger boxes containing candy, cartons of cigarettes, and other good things. The army called these "sundries" packages.

"Dewey, how ya gonna be?" he shouted over the roar of the chopper. "Ya took out everybody's hooch on the whole friggin' base!"

"So shoot the pilot, not me!" Dewey shouted back, his words sucked up and scattered by the whining, high-pitched roar of the chopper's takeoff. "I was just along for the ride."

They squatted, shielding their faces from gritty dust clouds driven by the chopper's rotor wash, briefly losing sight of each other in the resulting sandstorm. As the stinging clouds of dust washing over them mellowed out, Dewey raised his head, watching the ship's nose dip as it gained altitude and accelerated rapidly over the wide valley.

He wondered if the pilot had a secret fear of being shot in the ass.

"What a friggin' mess," groused Ingland.

"Take it up with the pilot, my friend. I didn't have nothin' to do with it." Dewey watched the chopper fade into the sky, rubbing grit from the corners of his eyes and lips. "Guess ya can't really blame him, though," he added, grinning as he brushed red dust from his fatigues with his free hand. "The man's gotta ride with the wind."

"I'll roger that," Ingland said with a chuckle. Turning, he motioned Dewey to follow him down the winding, well-worn trail that crossed rolls of razor wire and led into the firebase. "It looks like ya got my job too. Ever since the CO heard ya was comin' back out today he's been makin' noises like I oughta start packing up my shit. Guess I'm going back to Wrong-Way Coleman's platoon again. Thanks a lot, ol' buddy." He looked back at Dewey and smiled. "Ya bring back any dew?"

"Of course, how ya think I gonna be? I'd never forget my brothers. Good red Cambodian buds too," he boasted as they crossed the last trodden strands of razor wire then skirted a perimeter bunker. "But what's the story on the big Indian? He ain't got no ammo, no weapon, no rucksack, no nothin'. I saw two MPs put him on a chopper back in Tuy Hoa. At gunpoint! What'd he do?"

"Jumped on the resupply chopper, day before yesterday." Ingland grinned. "Didn't say shit to nobody, just jumped on like he had a reason and rode back to the rear. They caught him trying to board a Caribou bound for Cam Ranh Bay. The man's dinky-dow. Thinks he saw himself dead."

"Whatcha mean, saw hisself dead? That don't make no sense."

"How you expect me to know? All I know is he thinks he's gonna die out here. He's convinced himself of it. Say," Ingland stopped and pointed at Dewey's ruck, "why don't you go get yer shit squared away with the CO then come back over and join us on our bunker. We sure could use a taste of that good bud. It's been awful dry out here for the last few days." He indicated a small collection of shirtless boonie rats hanging out atop a bunker, silhouetted against the burnt-off jungle beyond the 105 pits. "Something's up, too. We've got a platoon meeting scheduled for just before stand-down. All the platoon leaders are huddling with the Old Man right now."

"Okay doak." Dewey grinned, sweat dripping freely from his nose. "I'll see ya in about twenty."

The two young friends waved as they separated, Ingland's feet kicking up drifting puffs of red dust as he weaved around piles of empty 105 brass casings. Dewey turned to trudge uphill toward Captain Wilson's command post.

Ingland was about his same height and build, and the sun had baked his skin the same deep brown. He wore a black scarf identical to Dewey's, right down to the logo. Colorful strings of Montagnard beads encircled his neck as well. Only the hair, hanging straight and disciplined over his forehead, differentiated the two.

Like Dewey, Ingland was an RTO. Sometimes called "Sparks" in earlier wars, the RTO had an unenviable assignment. Radios drew enemy fire like warm bodies drew mosquitoes.

As an RTO, Dewey's job was to carry and operate the PRC-25 radio, often referred to as the "Prick 25" by those who had to hump its weight up and down the Central Highlands. Its waving antenna made the RTO a prime target for enemy gunners. The communist Vietnamese were well aware of the Herd's superior air and artillery support. Take out the radio and they eliminated all hope of resupply and fire support.

Being an RTO also left the trooper in close proximity with officers, most of whom frowned on the boonies rats' extracurricular activities.

Dewey was tight with Ingland and his other buddies. In many ways, these friends were his brothers. He knew he was willing to die for any one of them, should a situation ever arise where his death could help them live. He also knew, without words, that any one of them would die for him if the situation warranted. They watched each other's backs, could count on each other, and they all knew it. They shared everything they had, with the maybe exception of peaches and pound cake, a delicious combination found in two separate cans of C-rations. Those were treats to be bartered with, or just enjoyed; rarely shared.

If one died in battle, it was his buddies that wrapped him in his own poncho, laid him hard and heavy into the diamond metal floors of helicopters as their insides churned with suppressed grief, several days before the families of the dead would even know of their loss.

The men of the 173d were quite young for the most part. Many were teenagers who had no reason yet to shave, but were not afraid to mix it up with the VC or their NVA counterparts. They had proven their effectiveness in battle many times over and lived by a separate, harsher code in the bush than they did when in rear areas.

The bush was the great equalizer. Everybody shit in the woods and at least tried to work with everybody else. That was the first rule of staying alive.

Not all the troopers smoked pot in the field, but many did. Dewey and his buddies were absolutely convinced that marijuana was an aid in their fight to survive the rigors of jungle warfare. They argued that being high made them intensely more aware; that it helped them smell odors that normally would have gone undetected; to have seen that faint glimmer of a trip wire they would have missed while straight. They smoked their dew openly but mistrusted newcomers, fearing with good cause that they might be CID[18] agents or planted informers. They kept an eye on officers, sergeants, and snitches—but never let their smoking interfere with their job.

The first cracking shots at the start of a firefight sent a surge of adrenalin that neutralized the marijuana's effect. The adrenalin rush had its own surge of hyper-awareness, or so they believed.

While their enemy's savagery had warped all of them to some degree, they had also learned a grudging respect for his fighting prowess. Most didn't consider their Vietnamese counterparts to be human. To them, the "gooks" were very deadly animals, predators that hunted the troopers as the troopers hunted them. Months of living in the jungles like rats, never knowing if a sniper's rifle sights were right then resting on their breastbones, or if the ground under their feet wouldn't erupt without warning, had honed their own psyches into their own form of savagery. To survive, they learned to be as brutal and effective as their mainly unseen enemy. They became moldy shadows able to slug it out toe-to-toe with the hardest of the hardcore NVA. They were young, they were proud, and they were extremely lethal. And, in the tradition of their comrades of earlier wars, they would not abandon their wounded or the bodies of their dead.

All had heard the stories of horribly mutilated Americans whose bodies had been stripped of their gear, then hacked to pieces by the NVA. Some were survivors of the Battles of the Slopes up in Dak To the previous summer of 1967, where two whole platoons of the 2nd Battalion's Alpha Company were almost totally wiped out after walking into a large force of NVA on a narrow ridge. Many had

---

18 Criminal Investigation Department. Investigates felonies connected in some way to the U.S. Army.

been executed, shot in the head while pleading for their lives after running out of ammo and being overrun—all within earshot of the survivors in the platoon that had not moved out with them.

Rumor had it that, according to Vietnamese superstition, the NVA believed that they could not get into Vietnamese heaven without their heads being whole. That was the main reason some troopers took the ears of the NVA/VC they killed. The practice became an effective psychological terror tactic that put the fear of the Sky Soldier in the minds of their enemy.

Yet even this savage practice had its own moral code. One had to have a positive, confirmed kill to take ears. If no one knew who killed the NVA, or if bodies were found after airstrikes or some other action where a confirmed kill was impossible, then no one took his ears. In such a case, the troopers would booby-trap the bodies were booby-trapped and place a 173d patch on their foreheads—or if lacking a forehead, his chest—a calling card for other VC or NVA to find.

The situation of finding bodies that no one could claim as a confirmed kill happened more often than not. The Vietnamese were masters of the ambush, lurking along trails until an American force was centered in their kill zone, and then firing at point-blank range. Those troopers lucky enough to survive the first few seconds would hit the ground firing, hosing down enemy positions with all the firepower they could muster while inching into the jungle to neutralize the ambush. If bodies were found after these firefights, it was often impossible to say who killed them.

These were the enemy that made it to heaven.

But it was the humping most boonie rats hated the most. Rucksacks were not carried; they were "humped." Mountains were not climbed, they were "humped." Humping was clawing your way up near-vertical slopes with an eighty-plus-pound rucksack kicking your ass in sweltering heat that was often well over a hundred degrees in the shade and humidity that averaged eighty to ninety percent.

Humping was getting your water wherever you found it, no matter how foul. Humping was ringworm and heat rashes and dysentery and jungle rot that festered overnight in even the slightest scratch. It was not being able to fall out as diarrhea waters ran down legs. Malaria was as common as the ticks, leeches, spiders, and snakes that infested the rainforest. Almost to a man, the troopers hated humping.

But Dewey loved it. To him this was a mega-adventure, a challenge of his soul and spirit, more so even than jumping out of perfectly good airplanes. There were no sewer-rats here. These were America's best, and he was among them.

He wrote Karen Coleman a letter that night. *Someday*, he thought to himself, cramming it into a deep utility pocket, *I might even mail it.*

Dewey was already sweating profusely from the short hump up from the LZ. It did not surprise him to see the big Indian sitting cross-legged atop his inverted, camouflaged helmet, face in his hands, staring at the ground. A few yards away, the CO knelt over maps with the four platoon leaders craning over his shoulders and listening while watching his finger trail over this or that map.

Spanky, a mature young man who used to wrestle for some Midwestern university and now fulfilled the role as his CO's right-hand man, spotted Dewey while he was several yards away. He nodded in greeting but quickly placed a finger over his lips in warning.

Dewey nodded back and kept walking until he drew even with the big Indian. A full rucksack had somehow appeared at the Navajo's feet. *Must have left it behind*, Dewey thought. "What it is?"

he asked good-naturedly as he bent forward, allowing his helmet to drop off his head. It landed upside down with a metallic clunk as he shucked his ruck next to the Indian's and stooped to squat on his inverted helmet.

"It ain't here," the Indian answered, not looking up.

Fine; don't talk, thought Dewey. *I just want to have my meet with the CO, get down the hill, and we'll break out some of that Cambodian Red.* As he waited, he scanned the firebase. Heat waves shimmered off sandbagged bunkers. He could easily see why the CO had chosen this location. It was shaded by a mountaintop from noon on. The grass hadn't been baked down into the dust, though it had been tramped into a lush carpet. He was praying for a breeze, even a warm one, when the meeting finally broke up. The platoon leaders, CAR-15s dangling on shoulder straps, fanned out down the hill, heading for their own hooches to prepare the evening's briefings.

The CO turned toward Spanky, then saw the new arrival. "Dewey! Good to see you, kid! Glad to have you back. So, you still want to be my RTO?"

Dewey could think of nothing he would less rather do. He'd been hoping to avoid the radio if at all possible but was prepared to hump even Wrong-Way Coleman's PRC if that meant he could be with his friends. He had used his RTO MOS as an in, but he craved rifleman status "Uhhh, no offence, Sir, but I'd really rather join Mike as a rifleman. I really think I would be more use for you there, Sir."

"In a pig's ass!" Wilson shot back. "You're the best RTO I've got. Get together with Spanky and secure the code books. Ingland left the radio over there." He nodded toward Spanky, effectively closing the matter.

Wilson, a tall, big-boned man with a high forehead and ragged, dirty blond hair, came from somewhere in the mountains of Pennsylvania. He had huge hands that wrapped around a .45 caliber M1911 handgun like it was a tiny .38. He looked down at Dewey, ice-blue eyes twinkling behind Army-issue glasses. "Dewey, you're my RTO now, whether you want to be or not. That's just the way it's gonna be. You wanted this, you got this." Wilson gestured at the panorama of mountains and valleys spread out in surrealistic relief beyond the firebase. "You and our wandering warrior here can dig in together tonight. I want him kept in sight at all times. Spanky can watch him for now, but he's your responsibility from stand-down to stand-to. Remember," he growled, turning to level a thick forefinger at the big Indian, "you're restricted to this immediate area. Right up until we move out at 0600 hours!"

"Move out?" Dewey exclaimed, "What move out? I just got here! Alpha Company just took over this firebase! We're supposed to have it for a month! Not fair."

"Whoever said the U.S. Army was fair?" Wilson grinned. "You make sure you get the code books back from Ingland. Go ahead and scoot over to Coleman's platoon. I know you want to see your buddies, but make sure you're ready to move out immediately after stand-to in the morning." With that, the CO turned and started to enter his hooch but paused, half in, half out, his eyes smiling. "Dewey, it is damned nice to have you back with us, son."

"Yes, Sir," Dewey answered, unable to quite keep the dejection out of his voice. He retrieved his weapon, forced a smile. "I'm glad to be back. Ain't no place I'd rather be, Sir."

The bunker was shady and relatively cool, gouged out of red clay, roughly four feet deep by six feet by six feet. Sandbags ringed it, three or four high, stacked like large bricks. Flat steel-reinforced planks lay across the hole, supported two or three sandbag layers deep to form the bunker's roof.

An entrance crawlway angled down into the bunker's interior, where Dewey sat with a handful of other troopers. Fifty yards from where he sat in relatively cool shade, heat waves shimmered up from the dusty sandbags of another bunker. Sun-scorched, shirtless paratroopers, some wearing camouflaged steel pots, were busy retrieving poncho liners, poncho hooches, clothes, and personal effects while gesturing obscenely at the departing Chinook helicopter that had just dropped off a slingload of ammunition for the 105s.

"Guess that makes my arrival no big deal, right?" Dewey asked, exhaling a long, curling stream of smoke that collided with shafts of sunlight from the bunker's gun ports and turned a silvery-blue, eddying into dreamy veils.

"Ya blew down my hooch," Barfield drawled, his eyes heavily lidded behind cobalt-blue granny glasses. He reached a long, sweat-sheening, chocolate-hued arm to accept the pipe from Dewey. His face was the same dark chocolate color and his teeth gleamed as he smiled. "And ja ruint my cocoa, but we glad to see you anytime, Dewey. Or, more to the point—" Barfield paused, peering at Dewey over his glasses as he toked on the pipe until it glowed; a seed exploded in a shower of sparks and Barfield knocked his glasses off as he swiped at a small, orange coal on his cheek. "Or more to the point," he repeated, "we always glad to see yer dew, Dewey."

"I allus knew ya was sweet on me, Barfield," Dewey responded. "That's why I allus brings you presents like this. Speaking of presents, looks likes you guys been hittin' them sundries packages and C-rats pretty hard." Dewey waved at the unusual amount of trash strewn deep over the bunker's earthen floor. Residue from looted cases of Cs and unwanted items from large sundries boxes littered the inside of every bunker he'd peered into on his walk across the FSB.

"Naw, only just a little of this shit's from our raids. Most of it was already here. Them ARVNs are some thievin' bastards, they are, they are."

Ingland chuckled. "They had the whole perimeter when we humped in. Most of 'em gone now but there's still a platoon securing the eastern perimeter. Those four bunkers over there, ain't but eighteen of them. " He twisted around Barfield to point out the bunkers with the pipe. Dewey's eyes followed his arm, looking for ARVNs around the bunkers.

"Don't even believe y'all see 'em out and about," said Barfield. "Uh-uh. Those suckers do nothin' but eat, sleep, and steal." Barfield made little chopping motions, one hand after the other. "All day, all night."

"Yeah, Coleman figures they went through a couple pallet loads of goody boxes before we come in. I keep hopin' to see one of the skinny little bastards crawlin' out on the LZ after dark. I'd fire his ass up without blinkin' an eye. He wouldn't have ta worry 'bout Charlie!" Ingland spat, his eyes dancing with reflected light.

"These mofos 'bout as worthless as tits on a boar hawg," Vincent Fyle murmured from around the stem of Dewey's 'White Ghost,' the pipe Medlin had willed him when he'd left for The World. Fyle's face wrinkled into a chocolate frown. "And they got an attitude too! They scowl at me behind my back and call me 'Muy' under their breath. These gooks weird me out, man! Here I am, fifteen thousand miles from L.A., fighting their war for them! And these worthless gooks get on my case with uppity airs 'cause I'm black!"

Dewey's eyes opened wide, the whites irritated pink by the marijuana smoke. "You are!" he exclaimed in mock incredulity,

"An' all this time I thought you was just a bath-less paratrooper." Fyle's first name was also Vincent, and they had a running joke about being related to each other by first name.

"I'll bath-less yer ass!" Fyle hissed, smiling a cloud of smoke at the shafts of streaming sunlight as the others snickered.

"Hey Dewey, ya worthless leg, bring yerself up outta that hole!" The voice belonged to a shadow briefly cutting off the sunlight filtering down the crawl-way. Dewey recognized it as Oliphant, a tall, curly-haired muscleman from Portland, Oregon.

"That's right, Dewey. We all wanna see what an honest-to-gawd ghost looks like!" hollered one of the dark-skinned, thin-faced troopers with Oliphant.

"Fuckin' Hopkins!" Dewey exclaimed, standing to duck under the roof and out into the daylight. "How the hell are ya, boys? I see ya just as classy as ever! Ya smell like a buncha fuckin' goats!"

Barfield and the others followed him out, and within a few seconds Dewey was being hand-shook and back-pounded by boonie rats he'd left behind in the jungles several weeks earlier. These were his brothers. They came from L.A. and New York and small towns scattered everywhere in between.

Shirtless, sweating profusely, young troopers sprawled atop and around the red-stained sandbags, drawing pipes from grimy utility pockets and filling them with the potent marijuana Dewey had smuggled in. They swapped news of the field for accounts of exploits in the rear. They listened with rapt attention as Dewey detailed the last night's incidents, paying particular attention to an explicit description of his shower with Chai Co.

Someone produced a small transistor radio. A pleasant electric soul beat thumped out over the fifteen or so troopers gathered around Dewey's bag of herb.

The view from that side of the firebase was spectacular. It sat on one of the tree-lined edges of the plateau that dropped off steeply to the valley floor about eight hundred feet below. A river curved around the plateau like a narrow, ice-blue crescent that bisected the valley below. Miles across at its center and widest point, both ends of the valley were progressively narrowed by sloping, jungle-blanketed mountains and hills. Beyond these, a seemingly endless gathering of peaks marched all the way to the horizon.

Two tiny specks of glinting light, pulling vapor trails, appeared against the cloudless, powder-blue sky over the most distant ranges. The white trails billowed in straight lines on a course that would bring the two silvery points directly over the firebase.

"Must be they gonna hit that NVA base camp what Echo Raiders found yesterday inna valley," Barfield drawled, squinting into the sky. "That's the same place those 82s popped in from, too. Yep. Betcha we in for a show!"

"I heard about that." Dewey said, shielding his eyes to watch the F-4 Phantom jets now curving around and diving as they approached the far side of the base from over the valley. "Where'd they hit? How many came in?"

"Sheeit, one hit right over there. I was catchin' some Zs in the bunker. Like to took ten years growth off me." Hopkins said as he also craned his face skyward, watching the jets. Hopkins had a really important father, somehow; all Dewey knew was that sometimes Hopkins would read out loud his letters home to his dad, begging his father to use his powers to get him out of the field. But in a firefight Hopkins was always right up front, bringing the fight to the enemy. He was brash and rowdy but quite likable and a hardcore paratrooper. "Guess about seven, eight rounds come in all together. You know Durand got hit, dontcha?"

"Durand! No! Nobody told me Durand got hit! Is he gonna be all right?"

"Got hit inna stomach with a pretty good-sized chunk of shrapnel. Bled all over the place and was in a lotta pain but I think he'll make it. He was walking from the Redlegs' chowline, just liberated us some roast beef sandwiches, when the first round popped about ten yards in front of him. No one else got hurt. That's his blood on the grass right over there." Hopkins pointed to a dark red-black stain on and under a patch of trodden elephant grass some thirty feet away from where they sat.

Dewey got up and walked over to the stained grass as the first Phantom dived past the far edge of the plateau, seeming to disappear into the valley. Underneath, away from the sun, the grass was still sticky with semi-dried blood. Flies crawled over thicker secretions glistening under the grassy carpet.

He looked over at the small crater about ten yards away where the mortar round had exploded. The jet resurfaced, surprisingly loud, thundering skyward as the deep rumble of its strafing run trailed it. The Phantom's 20mm cannons sounded like an elephant ripping giant farts into the sky.

Dewey dug down into soft red dirt until he found the mortar round's tail fin. It was dented and burned but had tiny black Chinese markings stamped into the metal. He turned to carry it back to the bunker as the heavy crack of the Phantom's thousand-pound bombs shattered sunshine and echoed across the valley.

"Explain this to me," Dewey asked the group as he approached, holding up the tail fin. "How do these tail fins survive the explosion? I mean, the round's casing is all blown out from the blast, right? An explosion is a round ball of hyper-destructive energy, right? So how do the tail fins make it through the blast? Seems it should be blown back skyward, not have enough force to fall through and bury itself inna ground. I don't get it."

"Lemme see that," Oliphant said, reaching for the scorched fragment. "Yup, ChiCom. If we gonna win this war they better start bombing the north again. Stupid fuckers! Don't they know we fighting Russia and China by proxy? The stupid fuckers!"

"Proxy? Sheeit! Half the gooks we killed in Buon Ma Thuot were over six foot!" Hopkins spat, before sparking a bowl back to life with loud puffs. "Show me a Vietnamese who's six foot! We fightin' the damned Chinese now!"

Satch, a skinned, thickly muscled black trooper who humped one of the M-60 machine guns for Mike Platoon, spat in disgust. "It's the whole world against us; even our own people. Look what the faggot hippies doin' back in The World! Marchin' down the streets with NVA flags! They should be marchin' with our flag!"

The group fell silent as the jets thundered in, disappearing past the rim of the plateau like they were diving into the ground.

"Sure glad those guys are on our side," Hopkins murmured as a jet resurfaced, followed first by the huge, farting, tearing sound of its strafing run and then the soft crushing *whoomph* of twin napalm explosions. The humidity and pounding sunlight stewed the afternoon as they sat and smoked their dew, watching the Air Force jets work.

A swarthy, grime-streaked trooper named DeGrau, his eyes reflecting sudden anger, jabbed a finger at a small, rat-faced trooper of Puerto Rican descent named Florez. "What the hell are you doin' here? I don't believe I been sittin' here smokin' with this worthless scumbag!" DeGrau jumped up, shouting, glaring at Florez as if about to strike him. "I caught the slime in my rucksack the other day! He's a fuckin' pogue[19]! Can't even hump his own ruck. Said he mistook mine for his. That's total bullshit! He was lookin' to rip me off! Ain't the first time neither! This asshole's ripped off half my squad! We just can't prove it!"

Florez silently hung his head and thrust his hands deep into his trouser pockets. Satch spoke up in his defense. "That's a crock-a-shit and you know it!" he barked, stepping in front of the scrawny Florez. "Sure he falls a lot! Humpin' busts up all our backs, only look at the size of his'n! I trust him, ain't never ripped me off! If you can't carry a brother trooper's load when he's really hurtin' then what the fuck you doin' in the Herd?"

"I'm gonna fergit you said that," DeGrau answered. "I just love givin' up my own canteens of water to pour over that faggot every time he decides he needs a break and falls out with heat exhaustion! Heat exhaustion, my mammy's ass! And I know what he's been lookin' for in my ruck!" DeGrau turned back to Florez with an evil grin. "It's 'cause ya can't stand the thought of a Caucasian married to a Puerto Rican, ain't it? I know yer after the pictures! Tell me ya ain't and I'll gutcha right where you stand!"

"Cool it," Hopkins said, slipping an arm over DeGrau's shoulder and trying to steer him away. DeGrau resisted, glaring at Florez, who pouted but did not retreat. The jets made one last pass each and then sped out over the valley, diminishing to two pinpricks of reflected light trailed by vapor. Even DeGrau fell silent as the troopers watched them go.

As the planes faded over the mountains, Dewey turned back to the altercation between the two troopers. *DeGrau's right. I've seen*

---

19 This contemptuous term refers to rear-echelon troops who never saw action, also called REMFs in some parts of Vietnam. Knowing that RE stands for "rear-echelon," the reader can guess at the other two letters.

Florez fall out plenty of times. Also seen how just so happens, when we were humping the upper slopes during the dry season, when he fell out somehow his canteens were always empty and someone else would have to pour their own water over him. As every Herd boonie rat knew, if an attack of heat exhaustion was for real, it became necessary to lower the victim's body temperature to prevent brain and tissue damage. In the highlands, the blue lines of creeks and rivers were way downhill. Water had to come from someone's fat-rats or canteens. Many troopers doubted that Florez really suffered any more than they did, and they harbored ill feelings toward him as a result. *But I know what this is really about, and DeGrau's right.*

DeGrau had received several nude photographs of his wife a few weeks earlier and had shown them around. His Puerto Rican wife was a stunner, her long, fanning black hair and amazing body framing a pretty smile. Florez had seemed to become irritated any-time DeGrau mentioned his wife. *There's no way Florez mistook DeGrau's ruck for his*, thought Dewey, brushing at a drop of sweat that dripped from his hairline onto his lips. The gesture smeared a thin sheen of red sweat-dust over his face.

"They coming back?" Barfield asked himself out loud as he stared off over the mountains. "Sure as shit!" he answered himself.

Dewey and the others turned at the excitement in his voice and followed his gaze out over the valley. The two gleaming specks of distant reflected sunlight had turned and sprouted wings. "I do believe they gonna buzz us!" Dewey shouted.

"No doubt, will you look at that!" someone else yelled as the two Phantoms, their dartlike shapes approaching at supersonic speeds, hurtled toward them over the jungles on what appeared to be a collision course.

The first Phantom came in roaring like a thousand freight trains, its wingtip less than twenty feet from the bunker. It was only a few feet off the ground as it passed over the cliff edge; Dewey could see every little bolt in the fuselage, and both crewmen, with crisp clarity. The pilot peered at them through the black visor on his helmet and gave a gloved thumbs-up as the jet flashed by, now just inches over the red clay.

The troopers went berserk, DeGrau and Florez included, jumping up and down and *Eehaaaing!* all over themselves as the second Phantom screamed in and flashed by mere feet from where the first had crossed.

The two jets abruptly turned their noses skyward and spiraled, making an entwining pattern with their exhausts for thousands of feet directly above the center of the firebase. The troopers cheered and carried on like a bunch of sports fans celebrating. The previous argument vanished and did not resurface. The radio emitted a beautiful tune Dewey had never heard before.

Tiger had come up with excellent dew, no question. But as Dewey sat tingling with color, he found his eyes drawn to the black patch of grass where Durand had bled the day before. Chills washed up and down his body just under the skin in pleasurable waves that had just a hint of vertigo. He felt spooked but rolled with it, staring at the stain and listening to the words of the song that vibrated with the shimmering heat waves, whose notes seemed also to vibrate into his bones. *The song was Crimson in Clover, its vibrating notes filled his body with a tingling pleasure...* he couldn't remember hearing a prettier song, but he couldn't keep his eyes from straying to the stain on the grass for the rest of the afternoon.

Toward sunset, shortly after a successful raid on the Red Leg chow line—a privilege accorded them by the artillery soldiers after they had all threatened to sleep on guard that night—Dewey spotted Second Platoon's first lieutenant approaching. "Kill the pipes!" he hissed. "Here comes Wrong-Way Cohen!"

Everyone looked around for any incriminating material. Dewey tapped the White Ghost out against his boot and ground the hot ashes into the red dirt. Other troopers were walking over from nearby bunkers. It was late afternoon now and long blue shadows gathered in the nearby trees, around bunkers and gun emplacements, pooling through the valley like a flood.

Far off in the west, over the wrinkled basins of the Hub, one mountain slightly higher than its neighbors stopped a long streak of reddish horizon from a spectacular sunset that colored even the air they breathed. Dewey thought the light looked like something from a cartoon, a peach gold that lent a surrealistic glow to the world.

Cohen was a dark-haired Manhattan native of maybe twenty-five. Though very intelligent and sensitive to the needs of his paratroopers, he had a bad habit of misreading maps. He had led his men astray more than once, hence 'Wrong-Way Cohen.' The lieutenant waited patiently until everyone in Second Platoon had assembled, milling around the bunker, laughing and calling out to each other in loud, obnoxious voices. Cohen cleared his throat, sniffing the slight breeze, probably for marijuana. His chin and cheeks were blue-black from a day's growth of whiskers and his side utility pockets bulged with maps and papers. A CAR-15 dangled on a leather sling from one shoulder while a gold Star of David glinted from a chain around his neck.

He held the notepad in his hand aloft to get their attention, then started his spiel.

"First, the bad news: The rumors are true. We're moving out in the morning." He made a wry face and shrugged. "That'll be 0600 hours, immediately after stand-to." There was a chorus of groans, bitching, curses and hisses. "Listen up!" Cohen shouted, raising his notepad, pointing at the high peak. "That mountain—"

The chorus did not dwindle. Cohen paused again, and then shouted: "Knock it off! If you'll just contain your enthusiasm I'll make this quick and painless." Now the chorus ebbed somewhat. Cohen scanned them with a look he probably hoped was authoritative, then continued. "That mountain," he repeated, pointing again, "is officially designated as Hill Five-Two-Two. Intelligence has confirmed the presence of an enemy battalion operating either on or near its slopes. The call sign 'Tiger-Tiger,' or something in Vietnamese that sounds like 'tiger,' has been identified in transmissions MACV has intercepted. That is the code name for the Yellow Star NVA, our old sparring partners. You've all seen the patch."

A stark image of a dead NVA soldier floated to the surface of Dewey's mind and lay there, brains oozing out onto the ground. Rigor mortis kept the empty head raised as if the young Vietnamese were listening to something far off in the jungle. He flashed the image to black.

"Anyone who thinks this is gonna be a picnic better think again. Intelligence has also provided us with a detailed list of their strength and equipment, so listen up! We are facing elements of the 95th NVA Regiment, along with some elements of the 85th NVA Regiment and an element from the 172nd NVA, the 66th Battalion; yup, the famed Yellow Star NVA. They are armed, for the most part, with AK-47s and SKS carbines, backed by AK-50s, PKK thirty-calibers, anti-aircraft heavy machine guns, B-40 rockets, ChiCom grenades, 62mm and 82mm mortar tubes, and are believed to have recently acquired several 122mm rocket batteries. Their man strength is estimated to be between 400 and 600 men, all hardcore NVA. They have weapons and rice caches all over the Hub. In short, they have the equivalent strength to a battalion of ours, they are well-armed, well-trained, and they aren't going hungry."

He paused, allowing his words to settle, then continued. "High Command has given us four days to reach the objective, Hill 522, which is approximately thirty clicks away. That means we must average almost ten clicks a day. There will be no time for fucking off! If you cannot keep up, you will be left behind. We will be traveling company-strength and will be joined by one platoon of ARVNs; from the 47th ARVN, and yeah, they suck. There will be one platoon of about 20 of them traveling with us. I don't trust them either, so we will keep them sandwiched between our own platoons where we can monitor their actions. If they run in a firefight, take them out; they will be running their weapons to the NVA if they do run, so drop them. Hopefully this time they will fight. If not...well, we do what we must."

Cohen's eyes danced over his troopers. He could not have missed the number that shook their heads with disgust when he'd mentioned the ARVNs.

"Other elements under the joint command will pincer in toward the hill, they being the rest of the 4th Bat, with ROK and ARVN units. Every man is responsible to see that they have five days of chow and adequate ammo. Every man is to carry a can of ammo for the '60s. Got that, Hopkins?"

Hopkins did not react.

"Every man, no exceptions, not even the RTOs—and that don't mean just carrying an empty can for letters and your personal shit, either. Got that, Hopkins?" Hopkins maintained a stony face. "I will personally check all ammo cans before we move out. Well, that's it. Any questions? No? Good. You have—" Cohen looked down at the black-gold watch on his wrist– "thirty minutes to stand-down. I want all squad leaders at my hooch at 0500 tomorrow morning, before stand-to. Okay, gentlemen, that is all."

The lieutenant turned away from the murmuring of discontented voices to stare at the mountain, shoulders slumped. The twenty-five troopers of his platoon broke up into small groups and dispersed. Dewey walked up behind him and gently touched his arm.

"Dewey!" Cohen exclaimed, a tired smile crinkling his eyes. "When did you get back? No, don't tell me, you came out on the resupply chopper with the AWOL, that Indian kid."

"Yeah, I did. He's a strange one. But it's nice to see ya missed me. Welcome back and all that."

"Hey, Dewey, I'm sorry. It is good to see you, it's just that I'm so damn busy and got a lot on my mind." Cohen paused; Dewey could see a small muscle twitch near the corner of his mouth. "Looks like the Ol' Man has you tapped for his RTO."

"That's what I wanted to talk to you about," Dewey answered, falling into step with Cohen as the officer turned to walk toward his hooch. "I was really hopin' to join your platoon as a rifleman. Ya know I'm good, I got two confirmed kills and I can take point better'n most anybody! And who else crawls through them gook tunnels better'n me?" Dewey's voice took on an almost pleading tone as he continued. "Couldn't you talk to the CO? See if you could make a trade? Ingland would rather stay on as his RTO anyhow."

Cohen stopped, looking at Dewey with haggard eyes that might have been appraising or just tired. His gaze dropped to the two mummified ears dangling below the beads circling Dewey's neck, then back up to his eyes. "You really like it out here, don't you?" he asked, his voice a mixture of fatigue and mild disbelief.

"Yeah, I do," Dewey answered, eyes sparkling.

"You know, I can't figure you out, Dewey. Half my guys—no, scratch that, just about *all* my guys, I think, would kill to get a job on the firebase, be it berm guard or shit burning. Just what is it you like about humping the boonies?"

Dewey suddenly felt too stoned for the conversation; something in Cohen's words felt threatening. Struggling against a surge of paranoia, he forced out his deepest, most burning desire. "I want to earn the Medal of Honor," he stated flatly, his eyes boring into Cohen's. "And you can't do that by burning shit."

Cohen's eyes fell from his to the ground, then bounced back up into the sky, finally settling on the blue mountain in the distance. A few weak stars twinkled in the deepening turquoise and the sunset was down to a last streak of burgundy.

"No," he said quietly, staring at the mountain, "I can't help you on this one. The Old Man likes you." He paused, turning to look squarely at Dewey again. "So do I, but..." Cohen gave a non-committal shrug, again staring at the ears hanging from Dewey's neck before continuing. "At any rate, you are his RTO now. So you might as well accept it, make the best of it. That's not such a bad job, and Dewey—" the worry wrinkles returned to his Cohen's face, contradicting the smile he tried to flash— "don't do nothin' foolish out there, okay? There's nothing glamorous about dead heroes." Before he turned toward his hooch, he raised his arm with thumb and forefinger cocked like a gun and winked down the barrel at Dewey.

Thanks for nothing, Dewey thought, watching the rumpled lieutenant pause at the next bunker down to shout at a dusty boonie rat carrying an M-60 down into the crawlway.

"I don't be*lieve* this shit." Barfield said, turning to Hopkins and Fyle, who had relit pipes atop the bunker. "Here I've tried almost every possible scam to get my black ass out of this friggin' field, and this crazy mothafuckah be fightin' to stay out here. There ain't no justice, man. I mean to say there just ain't no justice 'tall."

"How ya gonna be!" Dewey asked in the same tone. "My first day back inna field and already I been called a leg, crazy, and all kinds of mothafuckers! Now is that justice? Here, catch." He tossed Barfield a lurp bag stuffed full of red marijuana buds. "No, don't bother to thank me, just grovel." He grinned again, saluting with the barrel of his M-16. "I gotta run and put up my hooch before it gets to dark to see."

"Thanks for the—"

A long burst of incoming AK-47 fire sent rounds bouncing across the firebase, kicking up dust like stones kick up water when skipped across a pond. One whined in front of Dewey, stinging him with dirt, impacting sandbags at Hopkins's feet. Dewey hit the ground and rolled, simultaneously bringing his weapon to bear on a nearby hillside in the general direction of the whip-cracking chatter of the sniper's AK. There was nothing to shoot at. He held his fire.

Troopers scurried for cover all over the base. Some dove into bunkers while artillery and mortar crews scrambled to man their guns. The whole north side of the perimeter opened up on the hillside and the chatter of M-16s, '60s, and the heavier thump of the quad-fifty developed into a deafening crescendo.

Red-leg crews cranked down their 105mm howitzers' barrels as other members loaded rounds into their chambers and still others yanked the lanyards. The big guns fired point-blank into the hillside and recoiled with a crashing *KAWANG! KAWANG! KAWANG!* HE impacts blossomed in black and red thunderclaps against the nearby hillside. Each crew fired five rounds before ceasing fire.

Dewey lay on the ground, knowing the sniper attack was over. He hadn't fired a round. Outgoing small arms fire tapered off to nothing. Adrenalin pumped through his veins. He felt his heart pounding against his chest. Smoke and dust hung over the smoldering hillside in a drifting grey cloud as a flock of white birds wheeled away over the treetops, their harsh cries hanging like berry stains on the aftermath of the afternoon.

"That son-of-a-bitch does that at least twice a day," Barfield spat as he emerged from the bunker. "Now just watch. They gonna spend a hunnert-thousand dollars worth of ammo on one gook, what's already five clicks away, by bringing in gunships and jet fighters in the morning. Then they gonna send out patrols. Goddamn boonie rat don't never get no rest. Patrols ain't gonna find shit neither. Never do! Not a bad profit for that gook. Cost him maybe one thirty-round mag of AK shells."

"This guy ever hit anyone?" Dewey asked, beating the dust from his fatigues, listening with one ear for cries of 'medic!'

"Yeah. Got hisself an ARVN a few days back. Shot him in the ass as he squatted over the latrine ditch out by the wire," Barfield said, smiling as he toked on his pipe. "Funniest thing I ever see. That ARVN low-crawled a nine-second hundred with his pants down bleeding out a brand new asshole in his left cheek." Barfield smiled again, his eyes twinkling. "Here, you want some of this?"

"Nah." Dewey answered, turning to walk away. "I really gotta get my hooch up."

He hurried as he walked, feeling suddenly vulnerable. He couldn't get the image of the villager out of his mind. The one who had come out to shit that morning shortly after Dewey and Balisma had wasted the last chicken in the small Vietnamese ville of Phu Hiep, just beyond the wire back in Tuy Hoa. He could see him running, his pants tripping him up, shaking his fist at their bunker. He smiled at the memory and felt a peculiar sense of kinship stir inside toward the sniper that had been harassing the fire support base.

Maybe, right this minute, the sniper's smoking some herb with his friends, snickering over sending a couple hundred paratroopers scrambling for cover in the red dirt.

The peculiar peach color had vanished from the air as Dewey reached the command post. To his pleasant surprise, a poncho hooch had sprung up next to his rucksack. The radio and its spare batteries leaned heavily against his pack.

I hate OD green, Dewey thought, wondering who had put up his hooch.

Knee-deep at this end of the base, the elephant grass glistened with sparkling drops of dew: millions of droplets turned to diamonds by a rapidly rising, almost full moon. The sky had lost all hint of color, and the air temperature was dropping. Dewey shivered, pausing outside the empty hooch to rummage through his ruck for his heavy wool jungle sweater.

I'll repack that tomorrow during stand-to, he thought, looking down at the radio as he dove head first through his sweater, coming out the other side face to face with the big Indian.

"Hi, my name's Bluestone," he said, not smiling, looming large in the moonlight. He offered Dewey a hand the size of a first baseman's mitt. "I put up our hooch. I'm sure you don't mind. I'm supposed to hang out here for the night and, well, the CO did kind of order you to keep an eye on me. Right?"

"Dewey," he answered, looking up at the big Indian. "My friends call me Dewey."

"Mine call me Blue," the Indian said, releasing Dewey's crushed hand as he turned to toss his rucksack into the hooch. Blue grinned and Dewey relaxed, noting the Indian had perfect white teeth except for one gold-capped front incisor with a crescent moon cutout.

"Well, for the US Government they call me by my reservation name, Timoteo Santiago, but my family name is 'Blue Stone that Holds All the Waters of the Sun.' Some government man shortened it to Bluestone when my great-grandpappy was running around the reservation sleeping in government-issued, intentionally diseased army blankets. I think my ancestors loved turquoise," he added with a laugh. "Now the boonie rats have shortened it all the way to just Blue. Progress." Blue shrugged. "You get high, Dewey?"

"Does the CO shit in the woods?" Dewey grinned back, pulling the White Ghost out of his pocket.

Blue had constructed their hooch well, snapping his own and Dewey's ponchos together and using tree branches to hold them up, forming a temporary structure the size and shape of a small tent. He had even "requisitioned" almost enough full sandbags to cover the hooch's rear entrance, and had laid down a row two bags high along each side to provide more than adequate sleeping protection for the night.

Dewey hung his camouflaged poncho liner over the entrance and huddled over the pipe to light it. Even a faint glow through the liner might give the sniper something to think about.

Blue's hand wrapped around the pipe, his face reflecting an orange glow as he toked the ghost to life. A seed exploded, showering sparks; Blue scrambled to brush the more offensive ones from his lap. "Seedy herb," he mumbled his voice high and squeaky from holding in as much smoke as his lungs could hold.

"Sure is," Dewey mumbled back, his voice as pinched as Blue's. He exhaled and reached to accept the pipe. "Would ya mind my asking why the MPs brung ya to the chopper pad this mornin'?"

Blue stared at him for several long seconds, face unreadable. Given the size of the man and the close proximity, Dewey began to wonder if he hadn't just really screwed up.

"I'd be willing to bet you think you already know the answer to that question," Blue answered, inspecting the pipe Dewey handed back to him.

"Everybody out here thinks they do. I've heard them talking all day but nobody understands."

"I only have three and half months left before I DEROS, but... I'm gonna die out here." Blue turned his face away, sighing a long, lonely sigh. "I know it. For a fact I know it, but I can't get anyone to listen, let alone believe me."

"I'm listening."

"Yeah, but you can't help me. No one can, or will. That's why I'm gonna keep jumping on any chopper I can what's heading out of here! I've gotta get out, Dewey." He looked across the hooch with his big hands spread wide, "It ain't like I really saw myself dead, like I heard some of the guys saying today. It's more like voices, like ancestral voices that have been trying to warn me, in my head. Aahh, fuck it, you don't know what I mean!"

"Sure I do." Dewey answered, in a voice that urged him to continue. "I mean I don't and yet I do. Talk to me, bro."

Blue looked haggard in the dimness as he reached a paw to accept the pipe.

"These voices are more like a feeling. Have you ever been talkin' to somebody and just before they said something, you had a feeling you knew exactly what they were gonna say, and then they said it? Well, it's like that. I know I'm gonna die out here but nobody will believe me!"

This guy's really scared, Dewey thought, looking over at Blue's acne-scarred face. Blue had apparently forgotten that he still held the pipe. Dewey reached over and gently removed it from his fingers. "That kinda thinkin' will getcha killed, Blue."

Dewey paused to swat a phantom mosquito noisily invading his ear, suddenly aware the hooch was swarming with them.

"Ya gotta psyche yourself up, positively, then follow through! Ya gotta make this all a game, and ya gotta realize it's the biggest game of yer life. A bigger game than any asshole back in The World could ever hope to comprehend. There was a black guy who welcomed me when I first arrived back in Tuy Hoa. He gave me the best advice I ever heard. I mean it really burned in. He said, 'There are only two kinds of soldiers in Vietnam, the quick and the dead!' I never forgot them words, Blue. To get out of here alive you gotta hunt 'em and know every second that they're huntin' you back. Ya gotta tune into the game so good that ya can hear 'em sweat and smell 'em think!"

Dewey let his voice stop on an earnest pitch. "In short, ya gotta stay high. Like a wise ol' paratrooper once tole me, there ain't no hope without good smoke!"

Blue looked down at the pipe in his hand and saw it had burned out. He tapped it empty against the side of his boot, then handed it back to Dewey. Sighing, he turned to roll up in his poncho liner. "Man, you're crazy."

I'm crazy? Dewey thought, swatting at another invisible buzzing. *I must be. I'm sleeping in the same hooch with this giant, stoned out day-glow*[20].

---

20 A day-glow was someone who went off the deepest of deep ends.

November 2nd, 1968

Fire Support Base 20 miles west of Tuy Hoa

Central Highlands

Blue tapped Dewey's forehead lightly with a forefinger, re-coiling in surprise with the muzzle of Dewey's M-16 instantly stuck under his nose.

"Whoa!" Blue hissed, loud as he dared. "Chill out, Dewey, it's stand-to!"

Blinking stupidly and still not quite awake, Dewey lowered his weapon and fumbled in the pockets of his discarded shirt for a Marlboro. "Looks nasty out there," he whispered in a croak, nodding at tendrils of mist creeping into the hooch around dripping strands of grass at the entrance. "Wonder if this fog's here ta stay or if it'll burn off?"

"Fuck it," Blue said, sitting on his inverted helmet and staring out into the fog with the same distant expression he had worn during the chopper ride of the day before. "I hope it stays. Maybe the CO will change plans and not move out until later. That would give me at least a shot at catching another freedom bird."

Dewey was tightening down the straps securing his radio under cloth bandoleers loaded with full M-16 magazines, claymore pouches, and fat-rats[21] when the prepare-to-move-out order came. As Dewey moved to take his place in line behind the CO, he waved to Blue. Blue didn't wave back and his face seemed to sag with sadness as he faded into the fog, flanked by two troopers from Third Platoon.

The fog didn't burn off at all. Rather, it seemed to whiten deeper with the coming of full daylight. It swirled across the plateau in varying degrees of thickness, sometimes obscuring everything or limiting visibility to just a few feet. Sometimes it became a pale, translucent mist of dawn with prismatic rainbows that danced over the 105 emplacements, fading them in and out of the fog like ghostly relics from another war.

They stood in rank for several minutes, smoking, talking in low voices among themselves, before the CO allowed them to drop their rucks and sit down. Charlie Company, also of the 4th Battalion, was scheduled to take over the perimeter and had, but was still understrength because its Second Platoon had yet to emerge from the jungle.

Dewey's radio crackled with a hush of static. From behind his left ear a tightly coiled black wire snaked over his shoulder, dangling from the hand mic he'd hooked to his shirt pocket. He relaxed against his rucksack on the dew-drenched grass. The fog thickened in a white-out swirl, totally obscuring Ingland less than four feet away. The mist quickly soaked through everything, even the thick green towel worn around Dewey's neck and over his shoulders, under the rucksack straps. He wore his helmet reversed to prevent snagging vines and branches, which in turn caused moisture to drip

---

21 Gallon-sized water bladders. Very heavy and very necessary.

down the nape of his neck with cold clarity. He could taste sweat in the rivulets that ran down his face and over his lips. The mist thinned again and Dewey saw spiderwebs of rainbows grow where the sun almost shone through.

"Alpha Zulu One, this is Charlie Zulu Two, over." His radio crackled the words in an unfamiliar Southern drawl.

Without removing the mic hanging from his pocket, Dewey pressed the send button and answered. "Charlie One, this is Alpha. Over."

"Alpha, we're just outside the first row of wire, crossing in. ETA two minutes. Don't fire us up. Over."

"Roger that, Charlie One. ETA two minutes. What is your exact point of entry? Over."

"We're passin' pallet loads of Cs. From memory, I'd say we are bisecting the landing zone, over." Charlie Company's RTO sounded winded, his words ending strained and breathless.

"Roger, Charlie One, Alpha One out."

Without releasing the send button, he fell into the relay role, calling the First, and Third and the ARVN platoons, omitting Second Platoon as Ingland was once again their RTO and had already alerted his squad leaders to Charlie Company's arrival. Wilson and Cohen, who had been conversing like wavering ghosts ten feet or so from where Dewey sat, had also heard.

The company commander shouted to Dewey. "Get 'em saddled up! First Platoon on point, then Second, sandwich the ARVNs with Third bringing up the rear. No smoking or talking. Ten feet between men. Let's do it! Move 'em out."

Dewey relayed the orders, receiving acknowledgments from all platoon leaders, then rolled over on his belly and used his M-16 to lever himself upright. Spanky helped him the rest of the way up.

Dewey looked at the 12-gauge Remington pump shotgun Spanky carried. "Why do you like that better than an M-16?" he asked.

Spanky laughed and shook his head as he patted his Remington. "Man, this is like carrying six claymore mines that I can aim anywhere I need to. I ain't a sniper, so I don't need the long-range shit. Everything happens close up anyhow. Dewey, I couldn't find a better weapon for stayin' alive in this war."

The last trooper in Second Platoon disappeared, swallowed up by a billow of white. The CO waited the ten steps, then moved out. Dewey followed at the same interval, balancing his weapon horizontally across one grenade-filled ammo pouch on his hip. He could tell by the way his back already ached that his rucksack and the Highlands would make his body pay dearly for the past week's stay in Tuy Hoa.

Spanky fell in behind as the company uncoiled itself and waiting pools of troopers snaked into the mist. The first wraith-like, grime-soaked members of C Company's Second Platoon materialized a few yards off to Dewey's left. Their eyes were strained slits, though their mouths were smiling. The first trooper still held a black-bladed machete in hand, his weapon casually crooked in one elbow. Now and then one of the troopers of either company would sing out a greeting upon recognizing a buddy passing in the mist.

Dewey was no exception. Less than twenty feet away, a short, swarthy, wide-faced trooper swirled out of the fog. His name was Dantowski, a medic. Dewey hadn't seen him for months, but they had trained together at Fort Benning's Airborne School, as well as jungle school in An Khe after they arrived in-country on the same flight. "Yo, Dantowski!" Dewey yelled from under his bobbing helmet as he struggled to keep up with his CO's shadow. "How ya be, home-boy?"

"Dewey!" the kid shouted in sudden recognition. He stepped from the file of C Company troopers, turning to face him as the gap between them widened. "You be cool out there, Dewey, my man! You stay low, Dewey! Stay low!"

Dantowski disappeared into the billowing fog again as they neared the stacked pallets of C-rations. Dewey didn't answer. Captain Wilson had turned to glare at him.

Dewey followed him through the last strands of coiled razor wire, deeper into the fog. His radio antenna, made of a flexible thin metal kind of like a short length of tape measure, waved over his right shoulder. As they entered the wall of dripping grey-green vegetation, Dewey reached up and grabbed the antenna, bent its tip down, and hooked it through a strap of his web gear. The NVA had enough of an advantage without giving them a map to the radio.

Collected water sloshed over them from large cup-like leaves. Hidden vines conspired with entwining branches to form "hold-me-back," "wait-a-minute," and "knock-me-down" barriers that more than once reduced Dewey to all fours in the mud. By mid-morning the sun won its battle with the mist, melting the fog to pockets of whiteness filling jungle-choked, narrow gorges and wisps of white rising wraith-like beneath dripping fronds.

As the sun heated up, Dewey rolled up his sleeves, choosing to expose his arms to cutting edges of razor-grass rather than suffer the heat with them buttoned down. In no time his forearms glistened under mats of bright blood. The grass cuts were no more serious than paper cuts, but bled profusely. At times the troopers all looked in danger of bleeding to death as bright blood covered their forearms in thick, congealed mats. Blood dripping onto the black stock of his M-16 gave him an idea: When he got home, he would buy a car in these colors. Burgundy and black. He thought it a beautiful color scheme.

By late morning they were still breaking through rough brush, cutting diagonally across the slopes toward the distant hill. Occasional flocks of birds erupted from nearby foliage, their white feathers and harsh cries startling against the jumbled, green-black background.

The rucksack kicked his ass without mercy. Exertion pounded blood through his temples, turning his face a bright red. His breath was coming in forced gasps when the column finally broke through to one of the many speed trails that wound under the jungle's canopy. It snaked through the underbrush, its surface trampled by tiny hoof marks of multitudes of small, red-roe deer. The trail was slick, but not overly so when level. The pace picked up, almost always downward now.

Sometimes the trail would dog-leg uphill and they would climb, clutching at finger-holds, over jumbles of black boulders lashed to the ground by generations of dead vines and tree roots. Often, the CO's boots would be directly even with Dewey's eyes and he would have to wait for the officer to move on before he could use the same mud-slick niche to advance his own progress. At times the jungle thinned into light green stands of giant ferns, waving lacy fans shot through with many jointed spears of shadowy bamboo that played host to a few flowering vines.

For all the heat and the heaviness of his ruck, Dewey's heart sang. He was in his element, the most intense of all hunts. Watching the last few troopers in First Platoon flitting through the grasses in full combat gear like alert ghosts, pride stirred in his breast. It overflowed into his arms and legs, giving him a surge of renewed strength.

Once again he wished he could hump this company through his hometown, just to show the people who were carrying the flag for them, in all their sweating, muddy, humping glory. He was a paratrooper, a boonie rat, and—with hot sweat burning in his eyes and lacerated forearms bleeding from a hundred elephant grass cuts—he felt like a bastion of American freedom. Looking around at the men he was about to enter the jungles with, he knew in his heart that Karen was in reach. He felt fully very worthy of her now.

On they moved, catlike, M-16s and other weapons at the ready, Dewey's forefinger lightly touching the outside of his trigger guard.

The trail seemed to vanish, disappearing at the edge of cliffs then reappearing far below to meander up the slope of the next hill. A small stream, very blue, reflected sunlight in scattered spots where it became visible through progressively plusher vegetation at the bottom of a narrow gorge. From where they stood, the next mountain was only a few hundred meters away, reachable only by crawling down deep into the gorge and then climbing up the other side.

Going down proved nasty. Vines kept tripping Dewey, or he would skid on muddy rocks, yet he never fell far enough to get hurt. There always seemed to be a rock to stop his slide, or a clump of vine-like vegetation to grab onto. The constant slipping and sliding battered his rucksack and its pack job. He didn't have enough hands or time to stow all the equipment that tore, twisted, and crept loose from his pack. He was in a dark, exhausted mood when they reached the bottom.

No one was prepared for what they found. The bottom of the gorge was like the bottom of the letter V, black bedrock carved out by the stream and overgrown with lush vegetation. The stream filled a deep, wide pool at the base of a waterfall that cascaded out of craggy black rocks; it thundered under a canopy of flowering vines forming a rippling mirror reflecting a blaze of orange-red orchids. Water also bubbled and splashed over the black rocks from several lesser springs. A few brightly colored birds, curious but seemingly unafraid, watched them from perches almost hidden by jade leaves.

The troopers started gathering there, awe-struck. This was paradise on a grand scale. Captain Wilson turned to Dewey. "Call up Logistics, tell them we got a man down with heat-exhaustion, then call back down the line, tell 'em to set up a perimeter and take thirty." The captain shrugged his rucksack off as he gave the order, let it drop behind him, then started undoing his web gear.

Dewey stood rooted, looking around for the heat victim but not seeing him. "Who fell out?"

Captain Wilson smiled. "Does it matter?"

Dewey shrugged off his own ruck, relayed Wilson's orders to all platoon leaders, and watched as the lieutenants set up a protective perimeter around the pool. They hung out there for half an hour while the artillery forward observer and his RTO, Spanky, the first sergeant, and the CO went swimming in the ice-cold water and enjoying the tropical beauty of the spot. Dewey did not join them, but wondered if the others in the company resented the Captain's picnic. Half an hour after the halt, they repacked and started up the other side of the black rock V.

By 1400 that afternoon they reached a wide, grassy plateau. There was less water on the upper slopes and the grass was less green and lush than before. Only a few twisted trees formed islands in the small plain of elephant grass that stretched for hundreds of meters over rolling knolls and gentle yet deep depressions. As they crested one of these knolls, Dewey was startled to see two large birds rising like giant black pheasants out of the tall grass in front of the point man some one hundred meters across the field.

"Peacocks," Spanky said, smiling in answer to Dewey's wondering, backward look. Dewey grinned through the rivers of sweat dripping off his face and watched the two huge birds winging away, screaming like women as they glided down the slope and out of sight.

At that moment the sniper opened up behind them.

Dropping as he looked back, Dewey noted with surprise how little distance they had covered. He could see the whole firebase laid out in detail, with men running for cover like ants; he could also see muscles ripple down the side of a shirtless artillery gunner as he cranked a 105 down to fire point-blank into the jungle-covered slope of the same hill they'd hammered the previous evening. As before, the sniper had fired only one thirty-round magazine into the base. The return fire could have sunk a couple of battleships.

He doubted that they'd sunk the sniper.

A few minutes later, Alpha Company was descending on a widening trail that vanished into the thick, triple-canopied valley below. A voice came up on Dewey's radio. It was someone back at the FSB, giving data to a dust-off chopper that Dewey couldn't yet hear in or on the air. The voice crackled over the radio, as clear as if he was transmitting from just beyond the next rise: "Neck wound, shock, heavy loss of blood, height five-seven, weight, 175-180. He's one of yer own, too. A medic."

"Roger that, dust-off. ETA approximately fifteen minutes. Standing by. Out." The radio went silent.

Dewey's blood chilled. He unclipped the mic from his left shirt pocket, depressing the send button. He kept his voice as low as possible, hoping that neither Wilson nor Spanky would hear the unauthorized radio transmission. "Zulu Foxtrot Base, this is Zulu Alpha One, do you copy?"

"Zulu Alpha One, this is Zulu Base. What can I do for you, over?"

"Concerning medic you have down. Is his name Kantowski, over?"

"Uhhh, wait one, over."

Captain Wilson half turned, stooped, adjusted his rucksack. He sent Dewey a stern look, but did not try to stop him.

"Zulu Alpha One, this is Zulu Base. Concerning your question, that is affirmative. Over."

"Zulu, this is One, roger copy. Out," Dewey signed off.

His feet felt numb, thudding into the ground as if they were themselves chunks of dirt.

He could see Kantowski back at Fort Benning, Georgia during Airborne training. Fighting to keep his weight within acceptable limits so he could graduate. Sharing the two whores bought when they snuck into Columbus on a Saturday night. The night Dewey had got so shitfaced drunk on boilermakers that Kantowski and another guy had to carry him back to the barracks. He remembered only snatches of the night. Fading in and out of a shower, fully clothed, trying to punch Kantowski's laughing face.

Then the slamming of the door that woke him, dripping wet on a top bunk, still in his dress greens, as the full bird colonel of the training brigade came in for a surprise inspection.

Kantowski, fading in and out of the mist that morning and shouting for Dewey to "Be cool out there, man!" Kantowski lying with a big hunk of his neck blown out after some skinny NVA had put a bullet through his throat.

"Bastards," he said aloud.

Captain Wilson heard but pretended not to.

By late afternoon they reached the valley floor. The trail now ran wide enough for a truck to pass over it. The jungle had become much more intense than it had been on the upper slopes. Spider holes and old VC or possibly even leftover Viet Minh bunkers alongside the trail became frequent, many of these crumbling with age. Everywhere one looked there were punji sticks of varying lengths, mostly averaging six to eight inches long and sharp on both ends. One end had been shoved into the ground at an angle, just the right height to impale a man's instep or shin as he walked; the other end had been fire-hardened and dipped in human shit. The trail itself was clear of human tracks, but the CO sent out flank security to cut down on the chance of ambush. One whole hillside, denuded of all vegetation by napalm, showed punji sticks set out by the thousands as if sown by seeds and grown there as a crop.

Wilson turned to Dewey, waiting until he caught up. "Get on the horn," he hissed in a stage whisper. "Pass the word down to take ten. Smoke 'em if they got 'em, but no talking above a whisper."

Thank God, thought Dewey, passing the word back to Spanky. He had been convinced for several hours that there was no way in hell he could make it another step. He searched the grass gingerly with his foot, making sure there were no punji sticks hidden there. Then he knelt, turning until he collapsed against his rucksack as it anchored him to the ground. He reached for a cigarette, mentally cursing himself for needing one.

Captain Wilson dug in his own pack, coming out with a can of peaches. Using the P-38 that hung from a chain next to his dog tags, he opened the can while looking at Dewey over his glasses. "You knew that kid back there, huh?" he asked quietly, "The medic back at the fire support base?"

"Yes, Sir, I went through jump school and came in-country with him," Dewey answered, thinking how awful a cigarette butt tasted after being sweated on. "I hope he makes it, he's a good kid."

Wilson attacked his peaches with a plastic spoon, nodding his agreement. *As COs go*, Dewey thought, *Wilson's pretty good. Most of us probably seem like kids to him, but he treats us like fighting men.*

Me? I'm not sure he knows quite what to make of me.

Dewey thought back to the morning, months earlier, when he had killed his first NVA soldier, getting a broken nose in the process. They'd found the NVA soldier dead, thirty meters down the trail in the direction the remaining NVA had fled, stuffed into an old spider hole by his NVA buddies, shot through the right forearm with two rounds. One round had hit bone and mushroomed into the man's chest, creating a four-inch wide crater where his heart used to beat.

The explosion had knocked him out, but he'd come to soon enough. Dewey had puffed up like a bantam rooster as the platoons under Wilson had established a skirmish line and swept over the bunkers and trenches of the small base camp. The NVA had carried off their dead comrade, but had stuffed his body head first into an old spider hole just 30 meters down their escape trail. Evidently they had taken shelter in the large trench while trying to save him, but that had failed. They had left behind his bloody khaki shirt and web gear, which held a sack of cooked rice, two canteens, and several ChiCom grenades. Accepting kudos from his comrades on his first confirmed kill, one that had broken the back of the NVA delaying team and allowed the capture of several the grenades and web gear plus the detonator to a thirty-five-pound claymore the NVA had hung twenty feet up in a tree. It had been aimed down at the gully floor where 60 paratroopers had been laying.

That evening, after Wilson had informed Dewey that the Brigade's 4th Battalion commander had expressed a desire to photograph the dead North Vietnamese soldier, Dewey had become fidgety. Finally blurting out, "Sir, ya know that dead gook down there?"

The question was so absurd and strained that the CO had instantly known something was wrong. "Yeah," he'd answered, staring at Dewey in the darkness. "What about him?"

"Well..." Dewey had found himself at a loss for words. "Well... well, Sir...he can't even hear."

Captain Wilson had understood at once. "That's just great!" he'd hissed. "The goddamn Colonel coming out tomorrow and you've mutilated the body. That's real fuckin' smart, Dewey. Real smart." He had paused, staring at the baby-faced trooper sitting next to the radio in front of him. "What do you propose to do about it?"

"I figure I should have an 'accidental' discharge." Dewey had answered. "First thing in the morning I could walk down there and have an accidental discharge. The Colonel doesn't know where the gook was hit. One M-16 round should just about take his head off."

"Then do it! First thing in the morning. And Dewey," Wilson had leaned close to his face, his words heavy with constrained anger and revulsion, "I want you to bury him, by yourself, no help from your buddies. If the Colonel still wants to see him then, you'll just have to dig him up."

The next morning, after stand-to, Dewey had dragged the corpse out of the old spider hole. He stared at it for a few seconds, lying there on its stomach, head held up by rigor mortis as if the dead NVA were listening for something way out in the jungle.

Dewey had placed the muzzle of his M-16 against the NVA's head and squeezed the trigger. Half the NVA's skull blew out, and a large lump of almost intact grayish-blue brains oozed from the shattered skull onto the thick green grass. He put another round through the other side of the dead NVA's head, but there was nothing left inside to mushroom the bullet. It exited, leaving only a small tear hole next to the wound made where Dewey had severed the ear.

Dewey had stuffed him back head first into the same rotting spider hole, foot-swept his shattered clump of brains in after him, then jumped up and down on the rotted logs with their covering of earth until the small bunker collapsed. Using his entrenching tool, he'd scooped enough earth over the grave to cover the depression and, knowing the NVA would be back to retrieve the body, buried a fragmentation grenade with pin removed and the spoon weighed down with a large rock. Covering that with a foot of packed earth, he then dropped a red, white, and blue Herd patch onto the grave.

The Colonel hadn't come to the field that day. His confession had been unnecessary. Spanky told him later that the Colonel was not coming out to photograph a body, but to pin something on Dewey's chest that he had earned but now would never receive. Taking the ear of his kill had incensed Wilson, and his Captain had wanted him to know this. That there were consequences to his actions. Big ones.

Wilson finished off his peaches, watching Dewey take long, deep drags on his cigarette, the two ears around his neck outlined by strands of multicolored Montagnard beads. "Get back on the horn and have the platoon leaders come up here, on the double."

Dewey looked up through the tangle of limbs and vines over their heads, noting streaks of crimson starting to paint their way across the sky. He began calling the three platoon leaders. Nearby, the artillery FO huddled over a crumpled, spread-out map. Wilson joined him, tossing his empty peach can into the thick grass along the trail. Dewey listened in on the Captain's conversation.

The CO had wanted to travel another klick that afternoon, but there was only about an hour and a half of daylight left. He decided to dig in atop a nearby knoll some two hundred meters away, covered with thick swale grass and wild banana trees it rose from the surrounding jungle like a shaggy loaf of bread. After huddling with the platoon leaders, he gave the order to move out. Within ten minutes they were digging in and setting up a perimeter around the knoll in preparation for the night.

Dewey liked the spot. Dead grass formed a thick carpet about a foot deep; sleeping would be comfortable. In less than ten minutes he had erected hooch using his poncho and dead branches. While Captain Wilson and the FO, Redding, planned HE cover for the evening, Dewey slipped across the temporary encampment to join his friends in Mike Platoon. They were dug in on the south side of the hummock, where he found Hopkins, Ingland, and Barfield getting high around an M-60.

"Hey Dewey, come catch a squat. How's life with the Old Man?" Hopkins quipped, not bothering to lower his voice.

"Fuckin' ay!" Dewey answered, sitting on a dead log as Hopkins handed him the pipe. "I can deal with it. The CO's not such a bad dude. I hate that radio, though; it's about got my ass kicked."

"Tell me about it." Ingland said. "That ruck of mine weighs more than I do. I heard about your homeboy getting hit back at the firebase."

"Yeah. We come in-country together. We graduated in the same class back in jump school."

As he spoke, the two Kit Carson scouts—ex-NVA soldiers, nicknamed Ding and Dong, who had come over to the US/ARVN side after becoming disillusioned with the war and the almost constant bombing they'd been subjected to—sauntered over, grinning like idiots. Dewey had had a special relationship with the ex-NVA ever since taking the ears of his first confirmed kill and pissing off Captain Wilson.

Most everyone on the gully bottom had watched the drama unfold as Dewey made his first kill. They could not see the NVA, but they'd heard Dewey fire and seen the ChiCom blast that blew him into the air and swallowed him up in a burst of blasted dirt, fire and smoke. At the time, his comrades had thought he must be dead. After the main body of the company had swept up the hill, and Dewey had confirmed his first kill, most of the guys figured he'd take the ears. After the 'accidental' discharge, they all knew why Dewey had to bury him.

So did the Kit Carson scouts, though they'd been really pissed at first, carrying on like Dewey was poison, calling him "numbah ten." For the rest of the afternoon, the ex-enemies had scowled whenever their eyes met his. The next day, perhaps considering where they were and who they were with, the Scouts had laughed about the incident. "You cocadile VC plenty good, god dam, you cocadile VC. Beaucoup numbah one!" they'd said, patting him on the back.

Now they grinned at him like idiots. "Dewey! Long time no see, for sure." Dong tittered, or maybe it was Ding. Dewey never could figure out which was which. He had started to believe, correctly, that it didn't really matter neither to the Americans or the scouts. "You numbah one! Cocadile VC plenty by damn!"

Ding reached out to accept the pipe that Barfield offered, chattering something in machine-gun Vietnamese to Dong, who laughed softly in response as he sat on the log near Dewey. Dong seemed nervous, peering into the jungle with sharp, probing glances. He waved the pipe away, looking at Dewey with a smile that the furrowed worry lines around his eyes and mouth proclaimed to be false. "You look troubled, Dong. What's the matter?" Dewey asked, toking on the pipe as he looked into Dong's narrowed eyes.

"Smoke pot, numbah ten," Dong said nervously, nodding all around at the jungle. "Beaucoup VC, maybe smell *cahn sai*." He seemed to let his nervous eyes linger on Dewey's gory necklace, then continued in a shaky voice. "All day we see foot prints. Beaucoup VC. I smell fish. Two times I smell VC!" His eyes got slightly wider as his look darted about the surrounding foliage again, shaking his head and repeating under his breath, "Beaucoup VC."

After Dewey completed his two hours of guard and radio watch he lay on his back next to his hooch, staring up at the stars. It was two a.m. and he could still get a few hours sleep before stand-to. But he couldn't get Dong's face out of his thoughts.

Dong had been scared, really scared.

He wrapped his quilted poncho liner around his body and snuggled into the dead grass. Dewey's tired, aching body started to drift into sleep.

As he went under, he thought he could smell fish.

November 3rd, 1968

The Hub—Central Highlands

Dewey opened his eyes, blinking into the smiling face of Rawlings, the forward observer's RTO.

"Top of the morning to ya, gorgeous. I woke you up for stand-to, but, well, you weren't exactly into the idea so I let ya sleep. If you want to eat before we move out ya better do it now."

Rawlings turned back to his coffee, stirring his canteen cup with a plastic spoon. "By the way, check yourself for ticks. This straw shit is full of 'em. Medics took five off me already. They still pretty busy. Some of the other guys are infested with 'em. They took twenty off Barfield."

Dewey groaned. His body felt fractured from his neck to his toes. All his muscles were in agony. He wanted only to close his eyes and sleep, but he knew better. Forcing himself to rise, he started dismantling his poncho hooch, squaring away his equipment. Then he opened a chicken and rice lurp, ferreted out an envelope of cocoa and a few packets of sugar from one of the ruck's pouches, and filled his tin canteen cup with water. He pinched a small chunk of plastic explosive off the one-pound block of C-4 he carried. Clearing the grass from a small area, he grouped a couple of small rocks around the tiny piece of explosive so he had something to set the cup on while the C-4 burned[22], heating his water.

As the water heated, he performed a quick body search and found one gorged tick with its head buried in his crotch. He also noticed his ringworm was back; time to see the medic again. Lighting a Marlboro, he encouraged the tick to back out so he could kill it, then munched out on the steaming chicken and rice. After washing it down with hot gulps of hot, sweet cocoa, Dewey started stowing his gear. The sun quickly burned off the few wisps of mist that clung to the foliage.

He had just finished packing up when the CO called for him. Within fifteen minutes of his waking they were back on the trail, Mike Platoon walking point, followed by Headquarters Squad with the ARVNs sandwiched in between. Lima and November brought up the rear.

For the first two hours they made good time, only pausing now and then to wait while the point checked something out, or to keep the line spread out while the point broke through heavy brush or forded a particularly steep ravine. By mid-morning they had run into a problem.

The point radioed back visual sighting of six or seven NVA regulars, about a hundred meters ahead of the point man. Mike's platoon leader, Lieutenant Cohen, sounded eager to sic his dogs on them; Captain Wilson vetoed the idea, and they took a ten-minute break to give the NVA soldiers time to clear the area. After that incident the CO decided to move off the trail, explaining to the platoon leaders that the success of their mission depended on surprise. He

---

22 C-4 plastic explosive was a standard field-expedient substitute for Sterno or "heat tabs" in Vietnam. When not confined, in small amounts, it burned without exploding. It also gave off no odor, unlike heat tabs, and was immune to the moisture that would ruin heat tabs. With the issuing of lurp rations, the 173d started issuing blocks of C-4 expressly to heat water.

didn't want to take any chances of betraying their position by getting into a firefight, being seen, or leaving tracks.

"What the fuck?" Rawlings muttered as they started to move out, following Mike Platoon into the thick, twisted vegetation off the trail. "Every gook in the Nam has known where we were since we left the damn firebase."

The going got tougher as they moved uphill away from the trail. Thorn brush, rippers, and vines became almost impenetrable. Mike was forced to keep changing point men every couple hundred meters, thanks to the exhausting work of fighting the brush. Even those in the middle of the file had their troubles. Everyone had a machete in hand, hacking at walls of vines and entwined branches of thick brush.

Around noon they broke for lunch. Dewey elected to catch a small nap instead of eating, but the radio chatter kept him too busy. He wound up breaking out a can of beans and franks, eating them cold and relaying messages from the CO between mouthfuls.

Then they were moving again and the day heated up. Dewey's legs were cramping as he humped his heavy rucksack over tangles of jungle-covered hillsides. Little colored lights danced in front of his eyes. His breath came in ragged gasps as he followed the seemingly tireless CO up one tangled slope and down another. The wait-a-minute vines stole every ounce of strength he could muster. Sweat dripped off his face like rain. *Airborne*, he thought, in an attempt to just keep putting one boot ahead of the other. *All the way, Airborne*. He repeated it over and over in his head, silently mouthing the words like a mantra. The lights danced brighter and then he was falling.

Captain Wilson looked back as he struggled to his feet and staggered forward, eyes glassy. "You okay, Dewey?" he whispered.

Dewey cracked a grin he really didn't feel, nodded. He dug deep inside for a source of energy he knew had to be in there somewhere.

The afternoon dragged on. Vines alternately tripped him up or knocked his helmet off. He found a thin reservoir of strength, exhausted it, then searched for another. Somehow he made it through the day, welcoming infrequent five-minute breaks then grinding out his half-finished cigarette into the red loam as they moved on. Every muscle he had was letting him know it was alive and not well.

They moved back down the slopes just before dusk, toward the valley floor and its network of trails. The CO concluded that the time they were losing busting through the heavy brush was not justified, so he opted for the truck-wide speed trails. Better to make good time then bust hump through jungle that even native critters seemed to have forsaken.

Back on the speed trails, Dewey started to feel as if he might make it after all. Every now and then he had seen a bamboo viper, their fluorescent green bodies severed from an overkill of machete blows, lying on or near the freshly broken trail. The snakes had fluorescent orange eyes and a vivid patch of orange under their jaws. They were called "one-steppers." According to boonie lore and the medics, one step was about all you would get if they were to bite you. They were that poisonous.

If he was ever bitten, Dewey figured he'd ask which way was America and take his one step in that direction. At least he would die trying to go home.

Then there were the spiders, some big as pie plates if one included their long, hairy legs. They stretched their webs between the bushes over trails, hoping to catch insects. *Or maybe birds*, Dewey thought, recovering from the shock of having a particularly large specimen, a hand-sized bright yellow and black spider with a body shaped like a torpedo, run across his face to dive off into the jungle bushes. Its web stuck to his head, face, and shoulders.

Late in the afternoon, while the CO was thinking of finding a suitable place to dig in for the night, a call came in from Zulu. Echo Raiders had found an abandoned base camp and were securing it. They were only two klicks down the trail. If Alpha pushed it, they could all dig in there for the night in a kind of mutual protection arrangement.

The CO decided to go for it, and the next half hour was pure hell for Dewey. Even humping down the trail was difficult with a full rucksack while traveling at a rate just one notch under double time[23].

They made it with time to spare. Echo Raiders was waiting to greet them, very happy to see other Americans after spending 36 days isolated in the bush.

Dewey quickly set up a hooch using Rawlings's poncho as well as his own, and tossed his rucksack into it. Carrying only his M-16 and a bandoleer of ammo, he made sure the CO wouldn't need him for half an hour, then set off to visit Session and his other friends in Echo Raiders.

The NVA, who had chosen this site for a base camp, had constructed it well. They had dug it into a hillside covered with tall stands of thin trees. Bamboo flirted with the upper slope and the whole area was covered with lush, soft grasses, knee-deep and sweet-smelling, like clover. The perimeter bunkers were large enough to hold four men each. There was even a complex of larger bunkers for cooking facilities, complete with small tunnels that ran hundreds of meters out into the jungle for dispersing the smoke from their fires.

---

23 While most non-military folks have heard this term, in the military to double-time means "to run."

The reason for the NVA's hasty departure was still in place. A single delayed-fuse 105mm round had exploded directly inside their command bunker, destroying it. Anyone inside when the round detonated would have been blown into a fine, bloody mist. It had probably happened weeks earlier. Rain and insects had erased any physical evidence of the round's human toll.

Dewey found Session over by the bamboo, smoking dew with five other guys from A Company and three guys from the recon platoon. They celebrated with a wild little dance, hugging each other and pounding on each other's backs. Session had also gone through Airborne and jungle school with Dewey. After they exchanged greetings, they moved down into the bunker with two others that Dewey knew well from partying in La Bah. He told Session about Kantowski's run-in with the sniper back at the firebase.

"Damn," Session said, staring through burgundy granny glasses at a twisted wax candle sputtering on a jawless human skull staring up from the clay floor. "Kantowski. Why, Kantowski?"

"Why not?" Dewey answered while trying to rub a cramp out of his left calf. "It could happen to anybody."

"Except you, right?" Session said, positioning the skull so Dewey could stretch his leg out.

"Yeah, except me," Dewey answered, taking the pipe as it came around to him. "I'm Superman, the man of steel."

"You're steel all right," Session laughed, his glasses trailing bright reflections from the sputtering candle. "Steel hurting from that rucksack. Aye, amigo?"

As they talked and smoked, Dewey pulled his wallet out and extracted Karen's photo, the one he'd taken of her as she ascended the stairs in front of him in high school. He looked into her large almond-shaped dark brown eyes which reminded him of Cleopatra and passed the photo around. "My girl back in The World," he called her. Inside, the lie cut his heart like broken glass, but he had no other photos to show. And he did want, very badly, for her to be his girl.

Session was much like Dewey in thought and spirit. He came from a small town in California, a rebel in a large, poor family. He had volunteered for this duty, preferring the adventure, danger, and freedom of the field to the military humdrum of the rear or even the relative security of a firebase. He stood five feet eleven but his rail-thin torso made him look much taller. He also wore a black band around his wrist and probably fifty strings of colorful beads around his neck. Months in the field without a break had burned off any fat. He was as well-toned as a healthy cougar and the equipment he carried made him one of the most lethal cougars alive. His scarf held the Herd patch, CIB[24], and paratrooper wings, and also asked any who read it: *How Ya Gonna Be?*

At ten minutes to stand-down Dewey hurried back to his hooch, his eyes bloodshot and his body aching. When he got to his hooch he saw it had been trashed. The ponchos lay several feet away on the grass and everything not tied down on his rucksack had been scattered. He was dumfounded.

That is, until on closer inspection, he saw the six dead bamboo vipers hacked into about fifty segments each.

Later, when Rawlings returned, Dewey learned he had un-knowingly constructed the hooch atop an in-ground nest of the fluo-rescent green, orange-eyed snakes. Rawlings had just flopped down on his poncho liner to write letters home when the first viper had shot up out of the ground less than a foot from his face. The rest

---

24 The Combat Infantryman's Badge, awarded to veterans of ground combat. For any observer of U.S. Army uniforms, the CIB immediately identifies its wearer as someone who has functioned well in meaningful action, just as the jump wings identify the wearer as a qualified parachutist who went through Airborne School.

had followed in rapid succession and Rawlings had left the hooch wearing its materials, then returned with a machete. While cursing Dewey's whole lineage, he had proceeded to hack the small snakes into little slices.

Together they rebuilt the hooch about twenty meters away, but only after checking the ground very carefully.

Dewey went on radio LP at midnight, woken from a sound, dreamless sleep by Spanky, who stayed awake just long enough to pass on the watch before he crawled back to his own hooch and passed out.

Half awake, his brain numb but starting to formulate concepts of night-guard reality, Dewey picked up his mic and started calling each platoon for their situation reports.

"Lima Zulu, this is Zulu One, sit-rep. Over."

The PRC-25's static was a soft crackling hush in the moonlight. Then the static paused, twice, as one of Lima's guards broke squelch with his send button in the accepted, non-verbal code of 'S'all right.' Dewey went down the line, even calling the ARVNs, from whom he got no response. He would have been surprised to get one; the ARVNs were notorious for sleeping on guard. They let the Americans protect them. All other units answered as Lima had, negative—except for Echo Raiders. They only broke squelch once.

That meant trouble.

Dewey came instantly awake, his heart accelerating, adrenalin flowing. "Echo Raider, this is Zulu," he whispered. "Do you have visual contact? If yes, break squelch twice."

The static hush disappeared twice.

"Echo, can you speak in whispers? If no, break squelch once." Nothing. Dewey, his heart pounding, stared at the radio for fifteen seconds. He was just about to call Echo back when he heard the static stop.

A very quiet voice came through. "Zulu, this is Echo. We have movement at about one hundred meters to our left front. We can see at least one lantern and hear voices. Definitely Vietnamese. If they continue on this trail they will pass below us at less than ten meters. Over."

Dewey's mind spun briefly before he answered. "Echo, If you have any trip flares set on the trail, crawl your ass down there, re-move and secure the wire. Stand by, Echo. Zulu out."

He dropped the mic and ran over to the CO's hooch. The near-ly full moon was a help. Wilson listened, then said: "Good look-ing out, Dewey. You better make that a universal order, have all the platoons haul in their trip flares. And have someone from Second Platoon crawl over and wake up those damn ARVNs." Wilson put on his steel pot and cracked his CAR-15 open just enough to see whether he had a round chambered. "I'll wake the FO. Tell everyone to hold their fire. I don't care if they think the bastards are gonna step on them. No firing!" Then Wilson was gone, trotting over to the FO's hooch.

Dewey returned to the radio and passed on the CO's orders. Taking the radio with him, he slipped into the ruined NVA command bunker, watching a dim light bobbing closer a hundred meters out over silver grasses and darker shadows of the moonlit jungle.

The file of Vietnamese proved to be Viet Cong, mostly garbed in black cloth pajamas and wearing straw, coolie-type hats. There were about a company of them. Dewey thought he counted over a hundred. Most were pushing bicycles loaded with supplies; only their point man carried a lantern and even that was mostly taped closed, allowing only a narrow slice of light to escape.

Probably looking for booby traps, Dewey reasoned. *That means they definitely know we're in the area and they're being cautious. Otherwise they wouldn't bother looking for booby traps. They know where their own all are.*

Wilson and the FO gave the NVA supply column about five minutes to move down the trail, then called in artillery. Thirty seconds later, the first white phosphorus round screamed in overhead, air-bursting three hundred meters away in the direction the NVA had gone. Thirty seconds later the barrage screamed in behind it, round after round blasting into the jungle. The pounding fire continued for ten minutes, shaking the ground and lighting up the jungle less than a couple of football fields away. Somewhere in the darkness a group of monkeys started howling, but the fuck-you lizards all went silent and stayed quiet for a long time afterwards. It wasn't until Dewey woke Rawlings at 0200 hours that he heard another one.

He went to sleep with the lizard's *Akkkk kk kkk Fahck You! Fahck you! Fahk you!* echoing in the damp, cool, night air.

November 4th, 1968

In the Shadow of Hill 522

Echo Raiders moved out immediately after stand-to, the fog swallowing them up before they hit the trail. It was as if they had never been there at all.

Captain Wilson waited until the mist dissipated enough to allow visibility for at least a hundred meters. Then Alpha Company moved down the trail, complete with its undermanned platoon of about 18 ARVNs, always in the direction of the mountain that was drawing ever closer over the treetops.

There were a few more sightings of small VC patrols. They waited them out, not even calling in the artillery, then continued in a fast-paced hump toward Hill 522.

Dewey's muscles still hurt, but the cramps had become less severe. His breathing came easier and his stomach no longer complained about the small meals of lurps and C-rats. He felt energy to spare and relished the feel of being part of an elite paratrooper unit, of being lethal. His M-16 felt a part of him and he yearned for contact. He'd hoped for it from the moment they'd left the firebase. At first, he'd just wanted an excuse to lie down and get out from under his rucksack; now it was different.

He wanted to kill them, those who were hoping to kill him; those little bastards who had shot Kantowski. He itched for that chance.

The night before, while counting the VC crossing fifty meters from where he lay in the ruined NVA bunker, Dewey had battled an almost overwhelming desire to open fire on them. They had that trail covered for over a hundred meters with claymore mines, at least four M-60s, probably eighty M-16s, and a variety of other weapons with more in reserve up the slope. They could have annihilated them with few casualties, if any. But he'd followed orders and watched in total frustration as the VC slipped away in the darkness. *I hope the artillery found them and their fucking bicycles*, he thought, which looked likely from what he saw. Still he felt cheated, like an opportunity had been missed in this war effort.

The trail was covered with tracks that looked as if a car had grown feet: the VC and NVA standard Ho Chi Minh sandals. Spider holes had become more frequent and the smell of cooking fish permeated the air. At times he could even smell the strong, sweet odor of burning marijuana.

Both Ding and Dong had become much more nervous, and when the company stopped for lunch, they reported to the CO. Dong was very fidgety, his brown eyes narrowed and watery. He always held his weapon, never shouldering it by the strap. "Berry bad," he said. "Beaucoup VC, beaucoup NVA. We too small." He shook his head, pointing into the jungle with his weapon while shifting rapidly from foot to foot.

Dewey and Spanky sat eating cold C-rats, watching and listening. "Think they'll fight?" Dewey asked, voicing a concern about the Kit Carson scouts that hadn't crossed his mind before.

"They will, what choice they got?" Spanky asked in answer, not looking up from his ham and mother-fuckers[25]. "Man, this shit is inedible!" he said, tossing the half-eaten can into the bushes. "It's the ARVNs I'm not so sure of. If they were Vietnamese paratroopers, I'd be less skeptical. But these guys are just regular Powder Puff assholes. I think they'll run. In fact," he said, standing up slowly and stretching, "I'd bet money on it."

By late afternoon the jungle had become more woods-like, fewer vines and less vegetation. Some areas seemed completely dead, moonscapes where nothing grew. The ground was cracked and dry with many large black rocks peppering the slopes and flatlands, reminding Dewey of late autumn in upstate New York. All the leaves had dropped from the trees, creating a crunchy blanket of red and orange. Every living plant was either dead or withered. The leaves crunched underfoot like kiln-dried corn flakes. A low hill near the trail looked as if someone had planted foot-long punji sticks inches apart over the whole thing where napalm had burned off the dried grass. They had been there a long time, long enough for rain to wash off the feces and the sticks to turn gray or black, but they remained knife-point sharp.

They traveled through the dead and dying areas for about three klicks; then everything was back, as if some invisible line had been drawn through the jungle. Banana trees with large, bent stalks heavy with half-ripe fruit thrust up out of the sea of thick, razor-sharp elephant grass. The usual menagerie of vines and leafy plants hid the ground beneath the trees.

---

25 A meal of lima beans mixed in with some chunks of ham in some kind of sauce that turned most GIs' stomachs.

Dewey wondered what had killed the jungle behind them. *Must not get enough water for some reason*, he thought, reaching up to grab hold of a sapling to pull himself up a steep, muddy bank.

Still, it was strange. *Damn strange.*

They reached the last hill of any size before 522 shortly after six that afternoon. The hummock had only three or four clumps of stunted trees and was covered with chest-deep, thickly entwined grass that their jungle boots quickly trod down into brown mud that oozed dirty water beneath their feet. Like so many other places in the area that were easily defended, it was pockmarked with old bunkers in various stages of decay. Rusted C-ration cans littered the area around them, mute proof of earlier visits by GIs.

Hill 522 loomed in front of them, now less than half a day's humping away. It hung against the sky, brooding over lesser peaks and the wide valley. Thick jungle encrusted its flanks, thinning, finally disappearing altogether near the summit.

The mountain derived its numeric name from military charts fisting it as five hundred and twenty-two meters above sea level, but it was much higher from its base. The valley they called the Hub was the confluence of several rivers that looked from above like spokes of a wheel. It was actually several hundred feet below sea level. As Dewey estimated it, that made Hill 522 at least eight or nine hundred meters high from base to summit. The humping would be quite a bit longer, up steep slopes amounting to several miles of incline covered with boulders and jungle.

Like most of the other troopers, Dewey spent the rest of the fading daylight writing letters. There was something in the air, a foreboding that tingled in his nerves like a sharp, quivering musical note. Tomorrow they would climb the mountain. Dewey, along with everyone else, had a gut feeling that they would find what they were looking for there: the 66th NVA, the Yellow Star battalion, hardcore and ready, dug in the slopes on or near the summit.

With everyone expecting a major fight, many were setting affairs straight: telling family members that they loved them, not to worry, that everything was fine. Dewey wrote about the mountain; that he wasn't worried; that tomorrow should be the big one, that he was ready; that he was an airborne boonie rat, proud and strong.

Much later, Dewey lay on his back next to the radio, staring up at the stars. The sky seemed so much larger and clearer here than back in The World. The stars seemed far more numerous, a scattered explosion of dazzling beauty. The Milky Way spread out in all its glory. Every now and then a meteor would streak across the sky, some exploding in flashes of white light, some dying out in dimming showers of sparks.

I wonder if someone out there, someone or something, is looking out into an alien sky, right now, also far from home, just like I am.

A whisper out of the PRC-25 interrupted his thoughts.

"Zulu One, this is Zulu Lima Two, over."

"Two, this is One, whatda fuck? Over."

"We got movement below near the bottom of the north slope. Sounds like there's a water party down there filling metal canteens at the stream. Do we have permission to pop a few frags down on 'em? Over."

"Negative," Dewey answered, knowing he did not have clearance to give such permission, picking up a stone. He tossed it at Spanky's back where he sat hunched over talking in whispers with the CO. "Wait one, I'm putting ya on hold titi. Out."

Both Wilson and Spanky came over quickly, followed by the FO.

Wilson spoke with Lima's platoon leader, who reported that several positions could hear low voices murmuring in Vietnamese and the metallic clinking of canteens. The sounds had been continuous for at least ten minutes. Wilson told them to chill, that frags would give away their position. If the NVA mortared the small, grassy hilltop, a lot of paratroopers could get hurt. Instead, Wilson had the FO call in artillery.

Within minutes the valley floor was again hammered by invisible shells that screamed in out of the darkness. For the second night in a row, the 105s lit up the jungle very close to where they lay. The bombardment was deafening and some of the shells fell less than fifty meters away, showering the troopers with small rocks and clods of dirt. The smell of cordite and torn vegetation filled the air. After blasting the shallow valley so thoroughly that Dewey was certain nothing could have survived, the shelling stopped all at once. An eerie silence replaced the shrieking of shells and the heavy *KAW-HOMPH!* of explosions, but not for the remainder of the night. Now and then, the 105s would continue to fire salvos in their pre-assigned interdiction fire patterns.

Dewey felt like a kid trying to sleep the night before Christmas. Little tingles of excitement and thrills of expectation kept him awake for hours. He finally drifted off about 1:00 a.m., still dreaming about humping Alpha Company down the main street of his hometown in full battle gear, followed by shy maidens that looked to him with lidded eyes.

As he slept, his dreams changed. He dreamed of bamboo vipers and huge, yellow-black spiders that ran over his face. One had Cleopatra eyes.

November 5th, 1968

Approaching Hill 522, Central Highlands

No one talked much the next morning. Even after stand-to, most were quiet as they heated coffee, cocoa, and lurps. There was a little talk about the canteens they had heard clinking against rocks down at the stream the night before. The only other talking was the hushed whispering that rolled back along the stalled line like a bad rumor. It seemed the point man had found an undetonated, booby-trapped 105 round with a trip wire that blocked the muddy swamp-like trail they followed off the hill.

Dewey never saw the wire, even with the point leaving behind a man to indicate the wire so everyone could step over it.

The situation reminded him of jump school: being the eleventh man in line to exit the aircraft, seeing the door coming closer as each man jumped. He was right there, staring at the ground looking for the wire, and couldn't see it. He took a high, slow, very careful step over the general area that the young soldier was pointing at. He was too proud to admit he couldn't see it. He would rather have died.

Maybe he almost did. He breathed a sigh of heartfelt relief and hurried to catch up with his CO. But a twinge of guilt surfaced in his chest for letting his pride keep him from asking to better see the wire before stepping over it. He even thought it possible there never was a wire, that the point who found it, invented it for an excuse to stay behind and point at a nonexistent wire.

They'd covered half the distance to the mountain when they found the deer. It was a small, red-haired doe, obviously killed by artillery the night before. The jungle was so quiet they could hear the clouds of bluebottle flies swarming over the carcass from fifty meters away. Around the doe, saplings blazed white where shrapnel had torn off limbs and bark. The flies raised in a buzzing swarm as the column filed past.

Dewey thought of his father back in upstate New York. Probably got his deer picked out already, with hunting season only two weeks away. Suddenly the foreboding returned, stronger. As he passed the dead deer he thought the buzzing of the flies on the hot, silent air an omen. An evil, malicious omen.

Wilson called for a brief break, and moved up the line to confer with the artillery FO. Unfolding a map, they both hunched over it, using the FO's RTO to coordinate with the firebase, plotting pre-registered[26] fields of fire in case of contact on the slopes or the summit. Dewey saw that Hopkins and Barfield had fired up a bowl off to the side of the trail. Out of his CO's sight, Dewey joined them for a couple tokes.

Just as suddenly, the order came to move out. Dewey rejoined his CO.

Hill 522 was very steep, and long before noon, Dewey knew he was still very much out of shape. Stinging sweat poured over his eyes and the taste of dirty salt filled his mouth. His anticipation from the night before vanished in a red haze of pain as the mountain

---

26 Pre-plotted artillery can arrive more quickly and accurately, making the best possible use of the fire support.

kicked his ass. The jungle thinned to just a few scrub bushes and twisted trees struggling for survival in the thin, rocky, sun-baked soil near the top. Then they were there, pouring over the summit, collecting in tired groups around broken rocks strewn about 522's small double peak.

Their arrival was so anti-climatic that no one seemed to notice there was no battalion of NVA waiting to do battle. But the view almost made up for everything.

The whole Hub spread out around and below the hill in a panorama of jungle-covered valleys that seemed to stretch forever. A river, the same one at which they had heard the canteens being filled the night before, coiled like a long blue snake around the bottom of 522. It then curved off into the green lushness of the Hub, disappearing under a mat of triple-canopied trees, reappearing miles away in a wide curve that snuck around a distant peak.

Not a cloud disturbed the sky. The sun hung on the zenith, beating into the scorched earth and parched paratroopers as if it had some mad desire for vengeance. Dewey found himself wishing he had filled his canteens earlier that morning as they forded the stream, or at least that he hadn't drunk as much as he had during the climb. He had drunk so much water on the ascent that his canteens were all now empty, but he still had one full fat-rat that would do him for a while. He didn't know how long they would be up there, but there wasn't any water to be found on top of 522.

Not a drop.

Dewey sat against his rucksack, not even listening as Captain Wilson spoke with Zulu Command, wondering how he was going to dig into ground that was like cracked cement—and superficial at best, just a thin layer of dusty earth covering bedrock. Still, it felt good to just sit and relax.

From the little he had overheard of the CO's conversation with the Colonel, he gleaned that they wouldn't be going anywhere for awhile. They'd probably be regulated to blocking force status, meaning they might be atop that sun-baked mountaintop for several days, maybe even weeks. After the agonizing climb that morning and the back-breaking hump from the firebase, he welcomed the rest. He only hoped they wouldn't have to depend on 'water parties' for their replenishment. That would mean trips down the mountain carrying twenty canteens and four or five fat-rats slung on web belts to be filled in the stream they had crossed that morning, then humped back up the hill. Hopefully supply would send out water bladders by chopper instead.

The CO was still on the horn when Redding, who had wandered over to the very edge of the summit to observe the valley below, called out in a tense voice: "Sir! Come quick, I've got something here!"

Wilson signed off the mic and trotted over to join Redding and his RTO, Spanky close behind. Redding was peering through binoculars at the jungle below. As the CO pulled next to him, Redding motioned him to take the glasses, then pointed down the hill.

Dewey could see the FO's lips moving but couldn't hear the conversation. He was too tired to concern himself, and he would know soon enough.

Spanky came trotting back. "Dewey," he called out as he ran past, "get over to the CO, he needs the radio."

Wiping sweaty grit off his face with the olive-drab towel hanging around his neck, Dewey hoisted his ruck onto one shoulder and limped over to the edge.

Far below, at the base of the mountain, a wide strip of dead grass formed a football field-sized clearing separating the slope from surrounding jungle. Coming out of that jungle in pairs, exactly one minute apart, were crouched and running figures dressed in black and khaki. Thin grey-green bedrolls crossed their backs diagonally from shoulder to waist.

They had finally found the elusive Yellow Star Battalion, pride of the NVA.

Redding was relaying coordinates back to the FSB as Wilson snapped, "Tell First and Second Platoons to saddle up. We'll be going down in ten minutes. Then get hold of Thompson, have him report to me ten minutes ago."

That was when DeGrau showed up, his clothes dyed the baked, brownish red that matched the hilltop, asking permission to speak to the CO. Wilson looked up. "It's about pictures of my wife, Sir."

DeGrau was a no-nonsense trooper who had been out on LP for Firebase Lance, just two months earlier when hardcore NVA sappers had blown their way into the firebase. His voice shook with rage. "She's Puerto Rican and she sent me a bunch of nude photographs. That fuckin' Florez stole them! I know he done it! That lousy bastard's jealous 'cause he's prejudiced. He can't stand the thought of a white guy married to a Rican!"

Wilson nodded, but held out one huge hand. "Not now, De-Grau. I promise you, I will look into it. Thoroughly, first chance I get. I'll even shake down his rucksack myself." The captain turned back to his preparations.

DeGrau chose to press his point. "Shake down? Sheee-it! He'll have them gone by then! Thrown out somewhere!"

"I said later! That's an order, son!" Wilson snapped, pointing a thick finger at DeGrau's chest while straightening to his full six feet plus.

DeGrau stared at him for a few seconds, then spun on his heel and stalked off toward his platoon using Florez's name in association with many kinds of fuckers. Mike, Lima, and the ARVN platoon saddled up and stood in semi-organized groups, milling around while officers and men attended to last-minute details.

In the meantime, Redding brought in the 105s in a concentration that made the last two nights' displays look positively shabby by comparison.

The barrage lasted for over fifteen minutes. The devastation was awesome. Huge black-red fists of flame and smoke smashed into the valley below in rapid succession. A veil of dirty black smoke obscured the valley and still the flashes came: a pouring rain of high explosives as shells screamed in salvos a fraction of a second apart.

No one said a word, though they all probably had similar thoughts.

The big eight-incher[27] back in the rear at Tuy Hoa was firing as well, joined by 155s from a nearby ROK firebase. Shells were still pounding the valley floor almost half an hour later when Wilson gave the order to move out.

Waiting near the CO, Dewey watched as DeGrau, wresting point from his squadmate Oliphant, disappeared over the lip of the hill. He reappeared moments later on the bulge in the slope below, practically running downhill toward the clearing. A point man was not supposed to move that fast.

---

27 For comparison with the 105mm and 155mm fieldpieces, an 8" howitzer converts to metric at 203mm. Field artillery doesn't get much bigger.

"Shit!" cursed Captain Wilson. "I'm gonna have to give that bastard an Article Fifteen[28]. Okay, Mike, follow him. And send someone up there to slow him down!"

Dewey and the other veteran troopers understood, Wilson was worried about his point getting too far out front. He didn't want to come down the hill hell-bent, knowing a sizeable force of hardcore NVA was most likely in the area.

Wilson motioned Spanky to follow as the last man of Mike Platoon disappeared over the bare lip of the summit. Then he waited about ten seconds, slung his CAR-15 and followed. Dewey gave his Captain the same ten, and then hurried after. The rest of Alpha Company straightened, one by one, into a steady stream of paratroopers slipping over the edge.

As jungle closed over them, Dewey felt the familiar surge of excited anticipation overwhelm his exhaustion. If he thought of anything at all, it was to listen for orders that Wilson sporadically called back over his shoulder, orders Dewey relayed to platoon leaders up and down the file and the remaining platoon securing the summit of Hill 522.

They were going way too fast. Dewey found himself almost running to keep pace with his CO while trying to follow the faint hint of a trail meandering downhill through tangled vegetation. De-Grau was already three-quarters the way across the clearing at the bottom of 522 when the first troopers reached the edge of the tall, dead grass. Dewey could see him clearly, hunched under his ruck, weapon at the ready, stalking toward the woodline in long, angry strides.

---

28 Army punishment, considered non-judicial, at the officer's discretion. Could result in anything from a verbal warning to loss of pay or a short stay in the stockade. Less serious than a court-martial. In this case, DeGrau is doing something in a way he knows Wilson does not want it done.

No question, he's looking for a fight.

DeGrau had closed to within ten meters of several large ant-hills crowding the far side of the grassy clearing when a small, dark figure dressed in black hopped out from behind an anthill in a crouch and blew DeGrau backward with a short burst from an AK-47.

The Vietnamese hopped back as DeGrau flew through the air, his M-16 floating next to him in a slow arc. The upper branches of the tree line exploded in concentrated red and black fireballs as thumpers on both sides of the firefight riddled the jungle with HE. At the same moment that DeGrau's body landed in a crumpled heap, a crescendo of automatic weapons opened up on both sides of the clearing. Scores of M-16s and AKs, punctuated by heavy machine guns, filled the air with a deafening barrage that merged and swelled in volume: the unmistakable sound of a full-fledged firefight.

Faint cries of "Medic! Medic!" reverberated over the grass, sounding far away. Dewey had no recollection of hitting the ground or shrugging off his ruck, which lay in the grass several feet away. Invisible projectiles zipped and impacted around him. As he low-crawled through the grass over to his rucksack, he again thought of his mother. Green tracers, winking on and off in the sunshine, reached for him from the woodline as he fired back in short bursts, one hand fumbling to free his radio from the rucksack's frame. He had tied it down too well. With all the canteens, fat-rats, and other equipment it was impossible to jettison the heavy pack while leaving only the radio to carry. It was a mistake he would not make again. Now he was in trouble.

Spanky and Wilson were twenty meters off to his right, shouting for the radio. Green lasers snapped past his ears; something smashed through Dewey's pack, even as he knelt frantically tearing at the straps holding his radio. Rising to his knees, he redoubled his efforts as the radio slipped free. In a running crouch he abandoned his pack, radio in hand, flopping hard next to Wilson as .30-caliber rounds kicked up small rocks and dirt around them. He thrust the mic into his captain's hand.

Ignoring the incoming fire, Wilson rose quickly to his feet. "Let's go!" he shouted, drawing his .45 and running toward the woodline in a crouch with Dewey at his heels. The firefight raged along the edge of the clearing as First and Second Platoons closed with the enemy.

Wilson and Dewey were halfway across the clearing when they came upon a medic from Second Platoon, prone and not moving, with his medic's bag at arm's length. A very skinny blonde haired kid from Jersey, he had a strange-sounding name Dewey could never quite recall. Dewey's first thought was that the kid had been hit. Wilson stopped, seemingly oblivious to tracers and invisible bullets whispering past them. The medic looked up, his eyes wide with terror.

"They're calling for a medic over there! Can't you hear them?" Wilson shouted at the prone soldier.

"It...it...It ain't secure over there, Sir," the medic stammered, not even raising his head.

The firefight seemed to rise in intensity as did the frantic cries for a medic. Wilson aimed his .45 caliber at the medic's face.

"I'm giving you a direct order, trooper," snarled Wilson, cold steel in his voice. "Pick up that bag and get your ass over there or I'll blow your fucking brains out where you lay."

Pushing his bag ahead of him, the medic began a slow crawl toward the wood line. Wilson whirled and ran into the raging firefight, Dewey right behind him.

Shouts for medics still echoed up and down the treeline. One of Mike Platoon's M-60 teams hunched just inside the woodline very near the anthills where the NVA cadre[29] had been hiding in wait, the one that had killed DeGrau. Oschesky, the '60 gunner, kept pouring fire into a series of what looked like spider holes some ten meters back in the underbrush. He and his teammates Florez and Suggs had been hit by shrapnel from air-bursting M-79 shells[30] that continued to powder dead limbs overhead as Dewey and his CO flopped into the cover where trees met the clearing of grasses.

Wilson motioned for the handset, shouting orders that moved his force of troopers and ARVNs deeper into the jungle. Dewey concentrated his fire on the bunker that Oschesky was firing up. The gunner was bleeding profusely from his right thigh.

Wilson saw it too. "Give the weapon to your feeder," he barked, "and see a medic."

"I'm fine, Sir!" Oschesky shouted back as he cradled the '60 in his arms and rose to charge the bunkers.

He never took the step. His leg folded under him as though he'd stepped into a deep hole. He fell on his face with the M-60 beneath him. Florez stooped down and rolled Oschesky over, then snatched up the weapon and advanced into the brush, firing the '60 as he went. Suggs hurled a fragmentation grenade toward the nearest bunker. The explosion sent an AK-47 high into the air, followed by a black and khaki blur.

Again Wilson was on his feet and running, beckoning Dewey to follow. He ran down the line dodging incoming fire, shouting

---

29 In the VC and NVA, a cadre performed the same role as a political officer in the Soviet Army. His job was to set an example, motivate, and indoctrinate personnel in communist philosophy. Some were pretty good combat leaders.

30 It was not a given that the incoming 40mm grenades from these weapons were fired by US or US-allied troops. During the Tet Offensive, the NVA had captured warehouses full of weapons and ammo.

orders and encouragement. They came upon Cohen, huddled over a map with Redding, who was shouting into his radio.

A white phosphorous shell shrieked in behind them as the CO and Dewey sought cover. A white explosion full of green fire impacted the far side of the clearing where A Company had dropped their rucksacks. Redding shouted corrections into his radio, grabbing the map closer. Thirty seconds later another WP round burst out in front of them, in the jungle just beyond the NVA bunkers.

"Yes!" Redding shouted into the mike. "Battalion! Fire for effect! Pour it on, everything ya got! Fire for effect!"

The 105s shrieked over overhead seconds later, impacting the jungle in clusters of five rounds. Via the radio, Redding moved the barrage with the precision of a chess master.

Cohen's head jerked up with a start and his eyes opened wide. Dewey, trying to become one with the earth, followed Cohen's awe-struck gaze back to where the first round had impacted at the far edge of the clearing. A billowing cloud, hundreds of feet high and dazzling white, rolled toward them over the clearing, obscuring everything in its rapid advance.

"What the fuck?" Dewey exclaimed as the cloud rolled over them. Visibility was reduced to zero as the caustic cloud became a white-out.

"Tear gas!" Spanky shouted as Dewey tried to bury his face in the dirt.

Anyone who bothered humping a gas mask had left it on his rucksack. Dewey squeezed his eyes shut while holding his breath until his head began to pound. His eyes started to burn and then he had to breathe out...and in. He sucked in a lungful of gas, gagging as it seared sinuses and lungs. Sneezing and gasping, he could barely hear Spanky shouting something about a fifty-pound bag of CS pellets he'd seen near the trail just before DeGrau tripped the ambush. Dewey had seen the same bag, laying next to the trail where that muddy path met the grass at the edge of the clearing.

B-52 heavy bombers dropped these bags by the thousands. They were meant to rupture on impact, trickling the gas out over periods of six months. The theory was that if the Air Force dropped enough of these bags, they could make large areas of jungle uninhabitable. In the case of this particular bag, well, the theory erred. It hadn't burned at all until the short WP round had started a grass fire that in turn ignited the tear gas.

Spanky tossed a shovel to Dewey, who was bleeding profusely from both nostrils, swallowing blood to keep from choking on or drowning in it. "I'll watch the radio! Go back and bury that sonuvabitch!"

Firing had become sporadic except for the artillery, which continued to pound the jungle in front of their line. It took him several minutes to find the burning bag of CS pellets. Another trooper with a shovel found it almost simultaneously, and they hurried to pile shovelfuls of red earth over the bag.

Dewey's nose gushed blood with each breath as he staggered back to the wood line. The tear gas had stopped the firefight like an act of God.

Anticipating the Yellow Star NVA unit's retreat, Redding walked the artillery deeper into the jungle. The medic—the one the CO had forced at pistol point to attend to his duty—saw the gushing blood and now held a green towel to Dewey's face. Pinching his nose with the OD towel rapidly turning black as it absorbed blood, the medic lowered Dewey to the ground. After swallowing a lot of blood, the flow finally tapered off and stopped. His eyes burned, his lungs ached, and his throat felt raw as he watched Lima Platoon sweep through the jungle on line. The troopers looked tense, crouched and moving at the ready, sweeping the battlefield like stalking cats.

"How bad is it?" the CO asked Spanky, who was compiling casualty reports from the medics.

"One dead, seventeen wounded. Mostly shrapnel wounds from those damned M-79s. DeGrau bought it. I've already called in for dust-offs and HQ says they're gonna set up a mini-base up top. There are a couple of slicks and a Shithook on the way now."

"Good. Have Lima take the hillside and put out OPs. Mike's good where they are but get those ARVNs spread out on the left flank." Wilson turned to Dewey. "You all right?"

"Just a bloody nose, Sir. It's okay now."

"Good, run over and give the medics a hand. We can handle the radio for now."

The medics' treatment area was littered with moaning troopers. Field dressings were turning red, oozing over faces, arms, and legs. Doc Hartman, the head medic who never failed to lose his weapon during a firefight, was busy wrapping Oschesky's thigh.

This makes thirteen, Dewey thought, noting Doc was weaponless.

Suggs had also been hit. "I got that bastard, man!" he proclaimed over and over again. "I got that bastard."

Doc looked up at Dewey, motioning with his eyes for Dewey to go over by the tall anthills that stood like sand castles at the jungle's edge. "Give 'em a hand over there."

Four guys from DeGrau's squad, including Oliphant and Smokey, stood over his body where it sprawled between large, black, bloody rocks. After the NVA cadre had shot DeGrau, his buddies had crawled up and dragged him to cover in the rocks his body now sprawled between. It had been their voices Dewey had heard screaming for the medic who had lay cowering in the clearing. He had never seen a medic behave that way before. All other medics he had known were absolutely committed to their men in firefights, always responsive to the cries of "Medic." Until this one.

Looking at DeGrau's chest, Dewey knew the medic couldn't have helped him even with immediate action. At least five rounds had punched through DeGrau from the bottom of his right ribs to his left shoulder. The entry wounds showed as black spots on top of a thick mat of congealed blood covering his upper torso. His face was ash grey and his ice-blue eyes were wide open, staring as if in mild surprise at something in the sun beyond the azure Asian sky.

Dewey found himself drawn to DeGrau's eyes. *I wonder what he saw just before...* In a dreamlike state, he knelt to close DeGrau's eyes. *His parents don't know.*

He's dead, and his parents don't know. They'll wake up in the morning, eat breakfast...and they won't know.

"Goddamn medic wouldn't come!" Oliphant snarled through clenched teeth. He turned his head as his voice cracked and his eyes misted up.

"He drowned in his own blood, man." Smokey said, grabbing Oliphant by his shoulders and shaking him.

"He never had a chance. Fuck that medic!" another trooper spat, a tall and strangely chubby farm-raised youth whose rosy cheeks now burned red with anger and grief.

Dewey got up, speaking softly to all of them while standing next to Oliphant. "The CO and I passed the medic back in the clearing while you guys were yelling for him." Dewey said tonelessly, looking down at DeGrau. "The CO had to threaten him with his .45, and then he would only low-crawl, real slow, pushing his bag out front of himself."

"I swear I'll kill Florez, first chance I get!" the third trooper said, ripping DeGrau's poncho from his rucksack. He shook it out flat, like a green sheet, and spread it out next to DeGrau's body. "He stole DeGrau's photos of his wife. Naked photos! That's why Chuck was so far out front. He was pissed off. All because of that sandbaggin' mother-fucken' Florez! The medic's an asshole but it was Florez what got him killed."

"Wrong." Dewey said gently as he took hold of DeGrau's legs. "He got himself killed. I hate that fuckin' Florez too. But you know as well as DeGrau did: You can't push point like that and expect to go home. Not walking anyhow."

"Yeah, but that's what I mean," the red-faced trooper said in a strained voice as they laid DeGrau gently onto his green plastic poncho. "DeGrau was so mad he was lookin' for a fight. We knew the gooks were there. He wanted to fight! He was so angry he couldn't think straight. All because of that scumbag, Florez."

"Fuck Florez," snarled Oliphant, tears streaming down his face. "Leave him to me."

The four of them each took a comer of DeGrau's poncho and carried his body over to the medics. A fifth retrieved DeGrau's rucksack and weapon. Before they had carried him halfway, Dewey was struggling not to drop his corner, lest he inadvertently show disrespect for his dead comrade, despite the poncho's bloody slipperiness and the uneven ground. Out of nowhere, a thought surfaced in his mind. A simple disembodied thought:

Dead weight.

The dust-offs arrived a few minutes later. Three of them, in quick succession, without incident, taking DeGrau's body and the wounded away through clouds of the purple smoke the troopers had popped in order to help guide the medevacs to the landing zone. The dust-off choppers had come right up on their frequency. It was a huge comfort for the boonie rats to see the efficiency of those crews and to know they weren't alone.

The fire started by the short round had burned up several rucksacks, Dewey's included. He appropriated one from the pile of gear left by the wounded, replacing what he needed from other discards, as did other troopers whose rucksacks had also burned in the grass fire. The rest of the gear was thrown onto the resupply chopper as it tossed out cartons of C-rats, lurps, boxes of frags, and various containers of small-arms ammunition. Feeling like a ghoul, he searched the wounded's rucksacks for water—they all needed some—but the canteens he found were all empty.

He repacked his new rucksack and somehow was ready to go as the column started to move out along the wood line, turning right to follow a trail that doglegged deeper into the jungle. The CO sent Lima out on point this time and put the ARVNs between the headquarters squad and Mike Platoon. At first the ARVNs had refused to move out, but the leveled weapons of Alpha's grunts had encouraged them to reconsider. Still it was only after an ARVN lieutenant walked down their lines slapping each across their face that they took their place in line and started moving out.

Their eyes flashed with fear.

Dewey had taken about five steps, and maybe thirty troopers and the small platoon of ARVNs had turned up the trail, when the point element tripped a second ambush.

The CO turned, shouting for the radio. Dewey, who had hit the ground instantly along with everyone else, didn't waste time trying to get the radio loose from his ruck. He ran over to Wilson, who lay on the edge of the wood line twenty feet away, carrying his whole rucksack with him. Dewey dived onto the ground next to his CO and thrust the mic into his hands.

Two men down from where he lay, an ARVN was hit as he watched, the impact of the bullet pushing his prone body forward as if he were body-surfing in the red dirt. "We got snipers behind us!" Spanky yelled, firing back up the slope across the meadow.

Wilson barked an order into the radio. A few seconds later, a squad peeled off the wood line. They sprinted across the grassy clearing, crouched low, fanning out as they entered the jungle. Another squad followed after the first squad disappeared into the underbrush. Sniper rounds still poured in from across the clearing, their rounds splatting into nearby trees, whining off rocks, occasionally finding a man.

Dewey tore the radio free from the pack and slung it onto his back as a voice came up, clear and welcome, on the speaker. "Alpha Zulu One, this is your friendly neighborhood Dragon Fire. We've got some munitions for you. Just tell us where to put them. Over."

Overhead, two Huey gunships circled just out of small-arms range.

Dewey looked up at the captain, who was shouting orders. Dewey relayed the orders down to RTOs at both ends of their column: Pop green smoke to mark their line, and throw a red marker smoke where they wanted the gunships to hit. "Tell him to hit the red smoke!" Wilson yelled, running down the wood line toward the dogleg trail. Dewey followed him, shouting into his radio as he ran.

This fuckin' captain's gonna get me killed! thought Dewey, with dazzling clarity. Back to work, though. "Dragon Fire, this is Alpha Zulu One, hit the red smoke, I repeat, hit the red smoke! Over!"

"Roger, Alpha Zulu, I see your smoke. Find a hole, we're coming in. Out."

Suddenly Dragon Fire was there, just above the trees, a Huey gunship with miniguns[31] mounted on both sides blazing out thousands of rounds per second and twenty-millimeter cannons firing from the front, with rockets on board as well. Dewey could see the pilots through the Huey's windshield; he could also see the rockets as they left their pods.

Immediately behind the first gunship, another one came in firing 2.75-inch rockets and 20mm cannons. It came in so close Dewey could see the black-goggled pilots sitting inside.

They were too close.

The jungle on both sides of the trail erupted and rippled from the impact of thousands of minigun rounds as the ground shook from exploding rockets and 20mm shells. Men were screaming up and down the line. Dewey caught a quick flash of the big pudgy kid who had helped with DeGrau's body, his weapon in one hand and the collar of the medic at whom Wilson had felt it necessary to motivate at pistol point in his other, holding the medic up off the ground with one hand while bum-rushing him up the trail to where cries of, "MEDIC! MEDIC!" rose above the din of automatic weapons and shattering explosions.

That action would earn the heavyset kid a Bronze Star with V[32].

"Call 'em off, call 'em off!" Wilson screamed back at Dewey over his shoulder as he turned to run up the dogleg. "Don't let 'em make another pass!"

---

31 Six-barrel gatling-style machineguns that put out terrifying volumes of fire. Good to have on your side shooting at the bad guys.

32 The Bronze Star can be earned for non-combat reasons, but when earned for valor, it includes the V device.

Dewey was already talking to the ships, which had just begun another pass. He got through to them just as their fingers were tightening on their toggle triggers; both held fire. He saw the blinding reflection of the sun dazzle off the gunships' windshields as they swooped in, some rockets still ready in the pods.

One of the Kit Carson scouts, maybe it was Ding, staggered back off the trail and collapsed in the clearing. Weaponless, he gripped his left arm that hung limp and twisted, pumping jets of blood from a mangled and shattered forearm. Two ARVNs lay face down just up the trail, neither moving, bent and twisted, drenched in blood. The firefight swelled in volume again as Mike Platoon tried to penetrate deeper into the wood line.

The soldiers of the Yellow Star were well dug in. Their thirty-calibers caught the troopers of A Company from two sides while smaller caliber AKs laid a fearsome barrage of point-blank fire from numerous camouflaged bunkers and spider holes. Snipers had again infiltrated the hillside beyond the clearing.

The American counterattack bogged down, and then stopped cold.

Wilson paused, crouching in the middle of the trail. He scanned the jungle where bamboo merged with a tangle of vines, trees, and other vegetation. Lieutenant Cohen knelt behind a fallen tree with Ingland, trying to direct his men while firing short bursts into a spider hole less than twenty meters away. A thumper popped, followed by an explosion directly in that spider hole.

Hopkins came running out of the tall grass, eyes wild. "My weapon's jammed!" he shouted as he dove into the dirt next to Cohen. The lieutenant handed Hopkins his .45 and a couple of magazines. Hopkins abandoned his jammed M-16, turned, and disappeared back into the firefight.

Two Hueys were landing atop the hill, along with a Chinook double-rotor helicopter that was hovering just a few feet above the peak, a four-deuce mortar slung from its belly, the pilot waiting for one of the troopers on the ground to unhook it. Suddenly Hopkins came running back, hand cupping one ear like he was trying to hear something off in the jungle, "Listen! Hear it? Can ya hear it?"

"Yeah!" Cohen shouted back. "Sounds like mortar tubes popping somewhere out there!"

A split second later, the first cluster of a dozen rounds exploded near the summit of 522, downslope about a hundred meters. Seconds later, the rain of mortar shells obliterated the summit. The two Hueys lifted up and out of the clouds of dirt and black smoke from the barrage, tilting their noses down as they sped away. The Chinook wavered with its load as more explosions bracketed it.

Just drop it and go! Dewey thought.

The big chopper lifted straight up from dirty clouds of black smoke and debris generated by several near misses. It too lowered its nose as it climbed. Still carrying the big mortar tube slung underneath, it turned back toward the way it had come. A few seconds later Dewey could see it clearly, half a mile away, heading for the rear.

"Forget the mini-base!" Wilson shouted. "Let's press them hard. They'll be dropping rounds on us next!" The captain turned and sprinted up the trail, firing short bursts from his CAR-15 to his right as he ran. Dewey jumped up and followed him. More rounds impacted the summit as he watched his CO leap over a body sprawled sideways on the trail.

As he drew closer, Dewey recognized the body. It was Dong. He cleared the body on the run, but the sight burned into his brain. His system momentarily overloaded as shock waves surged through his mind.

Dong had been shot in the face, just below the nose. The round had exited at the base of his skull. Brains oozed down his neck and blood poured from his eyes, ears, nose, and mouth. His body twitched and spasmed laying sideways across the trail.

Dewey still followed his CO, but he was no longer all there. Something deep inside had snapped. He felt more vulnerable than he had ever felt before in his short life. His face felt hot.

In a rush, he felt as if there was already a bullet in flight headed for his face. Something that snapped now ran, silently screaming deeper into the darkness of his mind.

A fear above and beyond any nightmare he'd ever had swallowed him, then spat him back out on the trail and crawled up inside him where it spread through his limbs like ice water pumping through his veins.

Wilson ran all the way up to where the point had made contact, halting amid a scene of utter carnage. Several dead or dying troopers lay near the trail. Another, his feet hanging limply over the edge of a rocket crater, had taken a full charge of shrapnel from a rocket that had removed every other inch of his flesh and bone, from head to toe six inches deep; what was left had collapsed in on itself. Only by his blood-soaked jungle fatigues could anyone tell that this had been a human being.

Dewey forced his eyes away. The image lingered, burning brightly into a grey spot that tingled in his brain.

Someone close by was screaming "Oh my God!" over and over. Others lay still, crumpled and bloody, including Oschesky. "He's still alive!" the medic working on him shouted at Captain Wilson.

It was the same medic they'd found cowering in the grassy clearing during the first ambush; the same one Dewey had watched the chubby kid bum-rush up the trail, holding him out at arm's length with his feet off the ground at the start of the fight they were locked in now.

The grey spot tingled. His heart beat against his ribs like an animal trying to escape his chest. Dewey lowered himself until he squatted with his back against a thick tree. A hot slap of air burned his cheek. Chunks of bark bit into his face and he whirled, low-crawling to the other side of the big tree. A thirty-caliber opened up close by, tearing away the bark above his head in a shower of stinging pulp. He scrambled back to the trail side of the tree.

His eyes focused on a blood-filled boot in the middle of the trail. Its tongue hung out like a panting dog's, glistening with globs of shiny red-black blood. It had been unlaced.

No foot in it. Hope it's still where it should be.

Deep in his mind he could hear the boot laughing. Through the laughter, he could hear his Captain's voice, very far off.

"Dewey!"

He fled further into the grey spot. The boot was right to laugh. He was hiding behind this tree, right? *But on which side of the tree do you hide? If there is no safe side of the tree, where do you hide?*

"Dewey!"

His head snapped up. Wilson was kneeling in front of him. "Dewey. Are you all right? We got dust-offs coming but some of these guys can't wait. Get Zulu command on the horn. See if he'll come in. He's in that chopper up there." Wilson pointed skyward at the speck of a Huey circling the battlefield. "Tell him we got bad wounded that can't wait. Try to get him down."

Dewey tried, not surprised to see the tall, chubby kid, his left foot swathed in bandages and grimacing in agony, propped up against a nearby tree. *Must be his boot*, he thought, his own shock ebbing a bit.

Whoever had been screaming for God had stopped. A long, gurgling sound faded into a diminishing moan. A low voice, barely audible over the gunfire, called once for "Mom."

No more sound came from that trooper.

He managed to raise the 4th Battalion's CO on his radio. At first they agreed to come in and extricate some of the more seriously wounded, requesting marker smoke and reports on enemy incoming. Dewey popped a green smoke off the trail into a small, grass-filled clearing just large enough to accommodate the rotor cone of a Huey. As the helicopter homed in on the drifting, billowing pillar of yellow smoke, the pilot abruptly broke off his approach. Climbing rapidly amid an escalating surge of ground fire, the colonel calmly informed Dewey they had taken multiple hits, that they now had wounded aboard themselves, and that they were returning to Tuy Hoa.

The command Huey slick then turned and faded back toward the rear.

"Thanks a fuckin' lot!" Dewey yelled aloud, staring after the fleeing chopper.

Fifteen minutes later, a pair of passing Huey slicks returning from a resupply run overheard the radio chatter about Alpha having bad wounded that could not wait. They volunteered themselves as a dust-off service. They swept in on a pillar of yellow smoke billowing from the small clearing, but they too were driven off on their first pass, so the first pilot threw his helicopter over on the side and squirted away toward the clearing where initial contact was made.

Dewey knew that move. The pilot, obviously a seasoned veteran, was trying to trick the NVA into thinking his Huey had been disabled, to draw them through the jungle back to the clearing. He hovered there, pretending to be shot down, baiting the NVA to leave Alpha Company and attempt to take out both Hueys. When the pilots could see the NVA running toward them, they rocketed skyward, then safely inserted themselves into the small clearing to extract the wounded.

The fake crash worked, buying the pilots enough time to extricate all of Alpha's wounded. Wilson then consolidated what was left of Mike and Lima, pushing them into the jungle on both sides of the trail. Blowing bunkers with LAWs, they swept over the dug-in enemy. Redding walked the artillery closer to their lines, again enlisting the firepower of the big eight-inch howitzer back in Tuy Hoa. But the NVA had dug a network of trenches and a few tunnels, so the sweeps would stop the NVA firing only for a few minutes before infiltrating NVA would resume the high whip-cracking of incoming AK rounds. Other NVA, using ropes with meat hooks on the end, dragged away the bodies of their dead and wounded.

A couple of Phantoms shrieked overhead just above the treetops, cannons thundering. Each released two five-hundred-pound bombs an instant before turning skyward. Momentum carried the bombs like sinking black darts that vanished into the jungle. Dewey watched the slim black shapes fall into the jungle out front as empty brass casings from the jets' strafing runs fell in a clattering brass rain.

A hundred meters to his front, the jungle erupted into instantaneous domes of red and black. Shock waves flattened foliage, jolted the ground, smashed eardrums. Under that onslaught, the main NVA force finally broke and ran, taking their dead and wounded with them. Redding's artillery, the jets, and the gunships followed their retreat. Snipers and delaying teams continued to pin down the Americans with heavy automatic weapons fire.

As one dust-off settled into the small clearing, tiny holes began to pepper its fuselage. The ground fire swelled as troopers tried to protect the hovering medevac. Both door gunners raked the jungle over A Company's heads with their M-60 machine guns.

Four troopers, two wearing heavy bandages on their heads, struggled toward the medevac with Suggs's limp, bloodied body slung between them in a poncho. Other wounded men limped, crawled, or were dragged out of the jungle into the clearing.

The roar of incoming and outgoing swelled again. Two wounded ARVN troopers, hobbling together for support, dropped as one. Other wounded grabbed them. One was left in the grass, his brains literally blown out; a muscular black trooper with a bandaged chest slung the other over his shoulder. The first chopper lifted vertically, overloaded, both door gunners firing on full-auto barrel-melting[33] cover fire. The wounded hung out open bay doors like bloody spaghetti. The second ship immediately inserted itself into the tiny clearing, gorged itself with wounded, and followed the first.

Dewey watched the two Hueys pass over the trail where Wilson was shouting orders, just as incoming .30 caliber machine gunfire fire punched a door gunner backwards. As the gunner rebounded off the wall, a wounded trooper threw him back inside, grabbed the M-60 and continued firing.

Meanwhile Wilson consolidated his remaining men, then swept the battlefield for enemy bodies and equipment before executing a slow withdrawal to the wood line at the edge of the big grassy field. For the moment, the dead were left where they lay. The fight had raged on now for hours. Fresh air support continued to blast the jungle out front with HE, napalm, miniguns, rockets, and cannon.

---

33 Very intensive, uninterrupted fire. A machine gun's barrel will eventually glow red-hot and begin to melt if used for continuous fire. Crews carried spare barrels for this reason.

The incoming fire diminished to crackling sniper fire, sharp whip cracks that sent shirtless troopers to ground in unison. Almost instantly they would pop back up firing on full automatic, seeming to vanish again with the next surge of incoming.

Establishing a good skirmish line, Wilson again moved his company into the jungle, pushing the NVA delaying teams back, silencing snipers, retrieving Alpha's dead. The line settled in just beyond the point of the second L-shaped ambush's initial contact. Firing raged for several minutes, died down, then swelled up again. They could hear orders shouted in Vietnamese, audible even over the crackling of AKs and the din of M-16 and '60 fire. The NVA delaying teams had done their job. As Alpha Company swept forward, all resistance ceased with the exception of scattered sniper fire. Several further sweeps killed the remaining snipers or forced them to flee.

Wilson concentrated on setting up a defensive perimeter. He turned to Dewey and asked him to go through the dead trooper's pockets. That body still lay where a rocket had detonated at his feet.

Dewey complied, confronting a living nightmare. Shrapnel had obliterated the front of the young soldier; he had no facial features left, no dog tags around his neck, and his pockets were empty. Dewey relayed to Wilson that there was no way to say who this trooper had been. Turning away from the body, Dewey felt the grey spot consuming him. He was too numb to even try to hide his own horror.

The climbing of 522 and the long afternoon of combat had exhausted what remained of A Company. Ammo was low, and most of the M-60 barrels had overheated and warped. Water was almost nonexistent.

Dewey relayed Wilson's order to the top of 522. November Company was to send down a reinforced squad with resupply of ammo, M-60 barrels, and water. He could hear the medevac's thumping blades over his radio as he listened to November's RTO affirm everything but the water. They had been hurt badly by the mortar barrage, suffering several dead and many wounded. They would send the ammo but had no water to spare.

Reports from sweeping patrols confirmed the NVA had been badly bloodied as well. Spider holes were found full of blood, weapons, and empty 30-round AK-47 magazines. NVA web gear littered the battlefield. Although scores of blood trails showed where the enemy had dragged off their dead and wounded, no NVA bodies were recovered.

Now came the work of retrieving 173d and ARVN dead. A squad accompanied Doc Hartman in the process of gathering the fatalities. Dewey, digging a sleeping hole between radio duties, watched as the troopers struggled past him into the clearing with their poncho-wrapped burdens. Two at a time, the dead were brought to the large clearing's center where Doc opened the ponchos, examined the contents, then filled out yellow tags he tied securely to black boots that stuck out of the ponchos.

Dewey stopped counting at twelve, concentrating on encoding a message the CO wanted sent back to battalion. Even without continuing to keep count, he remained acutely aware of the struggling parade of the dead.

Wilson was knelt over a spread-out terrain map when Doc walked over. He awaited the captain's attention in silence, shifting from boot to boot.

"Yeah, Doc, what is it?" Wilson asked after several moments, not looking up.

"Sir, we, uh...we got a problem down the trail?"

"Son, I got nothing but problems," Wilson sighed. Looking up from his map, he removed his glasses and rubbed his eyes with the back of one huge hand. "What's yours?"

"The body up by the rocket crater. Well, he ain't got no face, no tags, no wallet, nothing in his pockets. We're having a helluva time IDing him. All we know is that he's a paratrooper."

Wilson looked away, closed his eyes and lowered his head. When he spoke, his voice was soft, gentle. "Take your list of the known dead and medevaced wounded; compare that with your malaria pill roster, then take a verbal, eyes-on account of the living. Your man will be the one who doesn't answer when you call his name."

"Yes, Sir," Doc murmured as he turned to walk back up the trail.

Wilson's head jerked up. "Just a moment, trooper!" he barked. "Where the hell is your weapon?"

"Lost it." Doc grinned through the grime and worry lines covering his face. "Some time at the start of the first ambush." He shrugged and started moving away.

"Not so fast! You lost it. This makes what? Thirteen?"

"I don't know. Maybe."

"Doc! You can't keep throwing away your rifle! The fuckin' gooks find them and use them against us. Don't you understand that!?"

"With all due respect, Sir!" Doc shot back. "I can't do my job with one hand full of rifle. I ain't here to fight. I'm here to try to save lives. From day one I've asked to be issued a .45. It'd stay in the holster and Uncle Sam wouldn't be losing so many M-16s."

"All right, all right. But try to find this one. That's an order. Uncle Sam is going to make you pay for every one of those weapons, so you look hard. Now get out of here and find out who that trooper by the crater is."

"Was." Doc answered softly as he turned to trudge back up the trail.

Wilson did not react to the correction.

Dewey had finished sending the message to battalion and was busily hacking at the red clay with his entrenching tool when he saw Doc returning down the trail. Four troopers followed him, staggering under the weight of a body bag.

He let the tool drop as Doc stepped off the trail to stand next to him. The four troopers continued past them to the rows of bodies laid out at the edge of the clearing. They watched in silence as the last of the dead joined the others at supine, poncho-covered attention.

"Who was it?" Dewey asked, his eyes fixed on the mounded poncho.

"Um, let me see. I can't seem to think," Doc answered, scanning a grimy sheet of paper he held in shaking hands. "Santiago, Private First Class, Timoteo Santiago."

"No. It wasn't," Dewey answered in a monotone as Doc turned his head to look at him.

Shock tingled down Dewey's spine, raising tiny hairs on his neck and arms.

He returned Doc's look with a half smile.

"His name was Blue Stone That Holds All Waters of the Sun."

He smiled again as he turned away from Doc's puzzled stare.

"But you can call him Blue."

Doc started to say something, changed his mind and moved on. Dewey swung his entrenching tool harder into the red clay. *Blue. But no dead gooks, at least none to see. And I do want to see them, piles of them.* Thick blood trails and spider holes full of gore bobbed up in his thoughts.

Not enough. I want to see every one of the bastards dead.

He had a vision of Blue, pleading with him back on the FSB, almost begging for someone to believe him; to believe that he was doomed. That he knew for a fact that he was going to die.

Another shock stopped his swing in mid-air. He let his entrenching tool slip from his fingers. The grey spot in his head danced with spots of color.

For the first time he knew; he was absolutely certain.

He could die. That he was the center to only his own universe.

That he could cease to exist in one bone-shattering instant.

And life would go on without him.

Coughing up a blood-flecked lunger, he spat it into the grass. He looked back to the rows of boots lying at odd angles where they protruded from grisly ponchos. The grey spot tingled until his whole body shook, causing vertigo. He wavered, then focused in on Blue's body bag. Blue lay in his poncho shroud, a green OD lump in a line of lumps that now humped the clearing together in death.

They were all so still. He half expected them to move; to try to get comfortable; to shrug off their shrouds so they could breathe. He reached down to retrieve his entrenching tool, stared back at the bodies for several seconds, then swung the bent shovel like an axe. Again and again, he vented his rage with each hack at the hard, red clay.

The resupply detail from November arrived at the far edge of the clearing as purple shadows deepened on the slopes of 522. The point man, flanked by troopers with belts of M-60 ammo slung over their shoulders and ammo cans in each hand, shuffled uncomfortably just inside the foliage. A loud, sharp whistle had alerted Spanky to their presence. Dewey dropped his entrenching tool to pick up his radio's mike, alerting the rest of the company to the resupply squad's entry position; then he took several steps out into the grass to wave them in.

Slowed by heavy cases of frags, M-16 and M-60 ammo, the twelve men trudged across the clearing. Dewey alerted both platoons to send runners for ammo resupply as the squad from Third Platoon arrived at Wilson's CP, exhausted but happy to be among fellow troopers again after their hair-raising hump down from the summit. Wilson sent the squad to reinforce his Second Platoon. Officers and their RTOs arrived for a hurried debriefing of the day's battle, just before stand-down.

Lieutenant Cohen, whose platoon had suffered the heaviest casualties, did most of the talking. After his line had turned up the dog-leg, they'd moved a hundred meters more or so up the trail when Cohen spotted an NVA soldier crouching in bushes just a few meters ahead and to the right.

"It all happened so fast." Cohen whispered, his voice a harsh croak. He stared at a spot over Dewey's head as he spoke. "The instant I saw that gook, I knew I had to get my men down. I mean he knew I saw him. We had eye contact and he had a roll over one shoulder and his AK at port. He tried to crouch lower and I should have shot the bastard. But...I wanted to get the men down fast, so I shouted for everyone to get down.

"I should have shot him. I mean, that would've got the guys down just as fast, if not faster, but I didn't and then they were popping out of the ground on both sides of the trail and all fucking hell broke loose. They had us cold. Some of the guys were hit as they dropped in that first instant. Then the gunships came and I thought maybe we'd be all right. When the call came down to pop red smoke, I...well...it was tough. They were really hugging our belts. A couple of thirties were chewing everything up. RPGs were coming in every couple seconds, and well, you heard how many AKs and SKSs were involved.

"We were pinned down and having a damned tough time even shooting back. To reach up and throw a smoke was to lose an arm. But someone threw it, must be one of the dead because I can't find out who did. The smoke hit a branch a couple meters off the trail. I knew it was too close as soon as I saw the smoke cloud. Satch dove for it, but took a burst in the chest. Then the first chopper made its pass. But it was Fryer who crawled out and got it, and tossed it to where it would do some good. But that rocket that took out Blue, also took out Fryer, it blew him towards the gooks, but then a B-40 rocket blew him back to our line. He got hurt pretty bad but he did get to that smoke and tossed it onto the NVA. He deserves at least a Bronze Star for that.

"Those rockets and miniguns hurt us bad, but the fuckin' gooks were really hugging our belts, so they got hurt too. I know the second gunship took out that .30-cal gunner...but it got Blue, too, with a rocket. Hit right at his feet. Same 2.3 rocket that wounded Fryer. Hurt him bad...but I think he will make it."

Cohen's voice cracked and he buried his face in his hands. Dewey saw the thing that had once been Blue, arms akimbo like a mutilated Christ, boots lying at strange angles at the edge of the crater. What had been Blue's face flashed Dewey's mind to black. Filled with guilt, he refocused on the young lieutenant.

"I should've shot that fucking gook." Cohen was shaking his head, slowly. "It'd been faster. I should have shot that fucking gook!"

Dewey no longer heard, nor was he listening. He was with the big Indian, back in the hooch at the firebase, smoking herb as he listened to Blue plead for understanding from the very man who would call in the rockets that would kill him.

"...and he was right." Dewey said aloud, not realizing he had done so.

"What the hell are you talking about?" growled Cohen, giving him an odd stare. So was everyone else.

"Blue. He was right. He said he was going to die out here. He knew it for a fact. And he was right. And I killed him."

"Dewey, Dewey, Dewey," Wilson said, rising stiffly and draping a heavy arm over Dewey's shoulders. "How do you figure you killed him?"

"With the gunships," answered Dewey, voice empty of emotion. "He tried to tell me that night back at the FSB that nobody would believe he was going to die out here. I called in the gunships. And now Blue's dead." Dewey stared at the ground.

"You didn't kill him, Dewey," said Wilson. "The smoke hit a branch. You followed my orders, just like the guy who threw the smoke. Everybody takes the same chances out here. Even if you do your job to the letter, you can die. You panic or fuck up, and you probably will die. It was an accident, a terrible fucking accident. That rocket could have found any one of us...or none of us. It found Blue. It wasn't you. It was an accident."

"Yeah," Dewey said softly, still staring at the ground. "Yeah."

Spanky had first watch near the deep fighting position hole they'd dug in case of attack, while Dewey crawled into his sleeping position and wrapped himself into his poncho liner. His M-16 felt cold and hard against his side. Within seconds he fell into a deep, dreamless sleep only the truly exhausted will ever know.

The earth shook under Dewey as heavy explosions nearby jarred him awake. The jungle off to his right was lit with the eerie green light of trip flares. Bright flashes of claymores exploded all around the perimeter. Smaller flashes from AK-47 muzzles spat out thousands of green tracers that crisscrossed the night just inches over his head as he low-crawled the five meters to the fighting position. The grazing fire intensified as he reached the hole—but it was no longer a fighting position. It was full to the rim with huddled bodies. He could see a pair of eyes staring into his, between arms, legs, elbows, and asses. With the green tracers crackling just over his head, Dewey sighed and quickly low-crawled back to his sleeping position.

With the firefight raging all around and the grid of green tracers still crackling just inches above his face, he rolled back into his wet poncho liner.

"Fuck it," he said aloud to no one. "Just fuck it all."

And fell quickly back to sleep. For the rest of the night, he did not dream at all.

November 6th, 1968

Hill 522, Central Highlands

He awoke with a start, his dew-soaked poncho liner slipping off his shoulders as he sat up. Spanky was heating coffee water over a flaming chunk of C-4 just a few feet away. The radio hushed with static where someone had propped it near the fighting pit.

A surreal mist drifted through the jungle and swirled over the clearing. Here and there other troopers appeared in and out of the vapor, wraithlike, as Dewey rose from his sleeping position. His whole body was stiff.

Avoiding his eyes, Spanky croaked a greeting.

Dewey retrieved his weapon from the folds of his soaked poncho liner, nodded back to Spanky. "How come no one woke me for my watch?"

"I couldn't sleep. No sweat. I covered everybody," Spanky answered, not looking up he stirred his coffee.

Four figures carrying a poncho-wrapped body, trailed by a fifth trooper, approached the rows of dead. They moved as if to a dirge. The four gently lay the body next to Blue's, then turned to disappear back the way they'd come.

The fifth stayed, head bowed.

Recognizing the grieving trooper as Disanti, a friend from Mike Platoon, Dewey stretched then walked over. The mist felt cold, damp. Disanti stood at the feet of the body bag, shoulders slumped, his weapon slung.

"Who?" Dewey asked softly as he stood close; needing, not wanting to know.

"Fyle." Disanti answered hoarsely. "Vincent Fyle."

Dried blood and red dirt streaked his face, showing the tracks of drying tears. Disanti's eyes were glazed, vacant, staring down at the body at his feet as if it were many miles away.

"We were eatin' Cs at the edge of the hole around midnight when a gook patrol tripped one of our flares. I blew a claymore on 'em just as we both dived into the hole. There was a lot of incoming. I could hear rounds skipping everywhere. Fyle tumbled in with me. I thought we'd both made it."

Disanti paused as his voice cracked. Tears welled, brimming until one ran down his cheek. "But Fyle was twitching on top of me. I struggled until I had him in my arms. There were claymores and frags going off all around the perimeter and at least a dozen AK muzzle flashes lit up the area! All within twenty meters of my hole! Blood was everywhere, man! He caught one just below his left eye. His blood was pumping out all over me, I tried to stop it...I tried...he died in my arms, never said nothin', he just up and died. I held him all night. All night."

Dewey looked down at Disanti's fatigues. They were black with blood. Disanti's eyes met his and locked. Nothing passed between them as they stared, too drained to console or cope, for several long seconds. As if on cue they both looked away, then down at the rows of dew-slick ponchos lying dirty and still in the morning mist.

The grey spot tingled, spreading down his extremities as he watched an ant crawl over a bloody boot to disappear under the poncho wrapping Vincent Fyle's body.

Dewey was busy repacking his ruck when the call came in from Zulu Command. The message was encoded and he was surprised to find his name buried in the letters as he deciphered the communiqué.

He was to be extracted. A Huey slick was already en route.

"But why?" he demanded of his CO as they sat, toe to toe, on slippery black rocks. "I don't want to go back in! I belong out here! Especially after yesterday."

But his words were not completely true. He did feel as if he belonged with A Company and he did feel a deep, primal urge for revenge. But the grey spot that weakened his legs and shortened his breath gave birth to another, stronger feeling.

He didn't want to end up wrapped in a blood-slick poncho.

"I really don't know, Dewey. Battalion wants you for something. They didn't say what. But I was on the horn to Charlie Company this morning. They're calling in RTOs from all over the Bat. And it's not a request; it's an order. My hands are tied. A chopper will pluck you out of here in about an hour."

Wilson rummaged in his rucksack as he spoke, pulling out a fifth of Johnnie Walker Red. Smiling, he held it up to the sun burning through the mist. The bottle seemed to glow amber from a light inside. "Here's to you, Dewey. Best RTO I ever had. I'm going to miss you, son. That's a fact."

Uncapping the bottle, Wilson took a deep drink. Squeezing ice-blue eyes tightly, he shivered, shook his head violently once, then winked as he held the bottle out to Dewey, a wide smile warming his face.

Dewey stared at the bottle, not reaching. What he saw was the dead and dying reflected off the glass.

Blue. What was left of Blue.

The Kit Carson Scout twitching on the trail as brains oozed from the back of his skull.

The grey spot tingled.

"I think I did all right yesterday," he pleaded in a low voice. "I don't deserve this."

He spoke haltingly, watching Wilson's face for any signs of rejection. Maybe his momentary freeze-up on the trail was it. Maybe Captain Wilson doesn't really want me around anymore after the mishap with the gunships. I still feel like that was my fault.

"I mean...I couldn't... It was...well, when I brought the gunships in on the red smoke I didn't..." He couldn't locate the words. Looking up at Wilson, his eyes watered as his voice broke.

"You did fine, Dewey. We were in pretty heavy shit. What went wrong with the smoke had nothing to do with you. I gave you an order, you followed it. The man who threw the smoke did too. A branch stopped the smoke. The gunships did their job. Men died on both sides. Hell, if you weren't so quick in getting the gunships to abort the second pass we may well have suffered far worse casualties. "

A tired smile crossed his face but not his eyes. He held the bottle out again.

"Here, take a slug. It'll do you good."

Dewey accepted the bottle, raised it to his lips, and let the amber liquid blaze down his throat. Wilson laughed aloud as Dewey lurched forward, coughing as he gagged on the fire that had rebounded off his stomach and was burning up into his sinuses. He held the bottle toward Wilson at arm's length while trying to gasp air into lungs that refused to accept any.

Chuckling, Wilson retrieved the bottle from Dewey's outstretched hand.

"I've never had any doubts about you, Dewey. Your actions yesterday were exemplary. I'm proud of you, son. But this order's on the up and up. I had nothing to do with it. Hell, if they don't reinforce us here, today, they're going to have to extract all of Alpha Company to rebuild."

Wilson swung the bottle back to his lips, took a moderate slug, then slowly re-capped it before stowing it back into his ruck. His eyes lingered on the rows of dead in the clearing. Just then Redding trotted over, obviously excited, his RTO hurrying to keep up.

"Damn. Sir! You're not going to believe this! The friggin' New Jersey is about to fire a mission for us. And guess who's gonna be their FO? Yeah! I can't believe it! ME! The friggin' New Jersey! And I get to call it in!" Redding was dancing with anticipation. "Better call in all the OPs and get everyone into a hole. They figure the gooks are on the slopes of the next hill back. Intelligence had LRRPs out all night. They say the Yellow Star NVA is definitely up there, licking its wounds. First salvo is coming in at 0830. Doesn't leave us much time. Damn! Me! And the friggin' New Jersey!"

Redding was about to have the privilege of a forward observer's career—even a lifetime. USS New Jersey was an Iowa-class heavy battleship from World War II. Its 16-inch guns could throw two-thousand-pound projectiles twenty-five miles inland. For comparison, the heaviest land-based artillery the troopers could normally call in was a battery of 8-inch howitzers, throwing shells of less than half the weight of those the battleship could fling. It was as if Redding were a parish priest invited to phone the Pope for guidance.

Dewey found himself wondering about the wisdom of this, given the horseshoes and grenades theory of near misses. The five-hundred-pound bombs of the day before had nearly deafened him. What would a two-thousand-pounder do, exploding just five hundred meters away? What if even just one round fell short?

How many paratrooper points for a near miss?

He lay face up in his sleeping hole, trying to see the shells as they passed over. He couldn't, but he heard them. They sounded like invisible jets. As they shrieked over, he cupped both hands over his ears and opened his mouth wide in a silent scream while incredible concussions beat over their positions, visible concentric lines of shock waves that flattened the elephant grass. The salvos continued for several minutes.

After the last hot waves of concussion passed over, a minute of deafening silence passed before the troopers began poking their heads up to look around.

When everyone was certain the barrage was over, the troopers got back to work. The pile of burned rucksacks grew as equipment left by the dead and wounded was gathered near the bodies. Weapons were neatly stacked; they scavenged all ammo, and water if any, from the rucksacks. Along the edge of the clearing, discarded AK-47 magazines littered the ground. Dewey again felt like a ghoul as he poured half-filled canteens into fat-rats for distribution. Personal effects of the dead and wounded were left in their owners' rucks; others in the rear would gather up their personal possessions for transport back to their respective homes in the Real World.

Smoke from the naval gunfire still drifted in smudgy patches as two Huey red cross-marked medevacs, their rotor wash dispersing green smoke, dropped into the clearing near the dead. Both pilots and door gunners gestured frantically for the troopers on the ground to hurry, but there was little need for the encouragement.

Everyone understood that, while hovering in the open, the choppers were prime targets for a mortar barrage.

Dewey was sent to help the squad from Mike Platoon load up the poncho-wrapped remains of their comrades. There was no time for formalities. They loaded the dead in haste, throwing the bodies atop one another onto the hard metal floors of the chopper bays.

It was backbreaking, mind-bending labor. The pile of bodies settled as dead slid down dead, their boots lying at odd angles. Pooled blood drained out from ponchos onto the diamond metal decks. As he helped toss a body onto the pile, Dewey had a mind-numbing thought that they should be gentle, should show some kind of respect. As the bloody green pile grew on the dust-off's floor, he lost himself in the grey spot.

Within a few minutes, the metal birds and impatient crews were loaded and on their way. He watched them rise over the jungle and shrink to tiny specks until they were gone. Then he turned back to the wood line, to the troopers, to say his goodbyes.

The clearing of the dead was empty.

Half an hour later, a single slick plucked Dewey from the clearing. He carried only his weapon and a cloth bandoleer of M-16 magazines. He left his newly acquired ruck and all his ammunition behind except the magazine in his weapon. As the chopper gained altitude, he was able to take in the whole of the battlefield.

The jungle surrounding the dog-leg trail had been cratered by 500-pound bombs and various artillery strikes. Napalm had blackened the area. The nearby hill Redding had pounded with the New Jersey's guns still smoldered. Hardly a tree stood on its slopes. If the Yellow Star had truly been there, they were with their ancestors now. Nothing could have lived through the ravaging inflicted upon that hill. Pillars of black smoke rose from the few limbless tree trunks still standing, dissipating into a cloudless, powder-blue Asian sky.

Minutes later the slick flared onto the LZ at the firebase. Just one trooper clambered aboard. It was Tree, the tall kid from Idaho. They hugged each other fiercely as the chopper rose in a hurricane of dust above rapidly shrinking bunkers and barbed wire.

"How ya be, Tree?" Dewey shouted as they settled in for the short ride back to Tuy Hoa.

"Been better!" Tree shouted, straining to be heard over the chopper's engines. "You all right, Dew?" he added, looking Dewey up and down, apprehension evident in his eyes.

Following his gaze, Dewey looked down at his fatigues. They were black with dried blood. "I'm fine! A lot of other guys ain't but I'm fine!"

"You look like hell!" Tree shouted. "They's even blood in yer hair!"

"Yeah, well, it got nasty out there! So what's up? Why are they pulling us in?"

"You don't know?" Tree stared at him, incredulous. Then he leaned close to shout into Dewey's ear. "Dewey, the commo-team was wiped out by mortars atop Hill 522. Green, Circus Boy, Ice-man...they're all dead! Vaughn lost his legs and Red got hit hard by shrapnel in his right shoulder." Tree backed off, his eyes full of tears, still staring into Dewey's.

Dewey stared back, mouth agape, the grey place growing until his whole body shook and his vision faded into a static of gray and flashing, multi-colored spots of light.

Tree's face slowly grew back into focus, blurred, and then Dewey could see clearly again. "You okay?" Tree's shout merged with the thrum of the chopper.

"Green? Iceman? Mann? All dead?"

Somehow the nickname "Circus Boy" now rang hollow.

Tree read his lips, nodding as he lowered his head close to Dewey's face. "You gonna be all right?"

"Yeah," Dewey said, his mind filling with images of dead friends' faces.

"Frenchy's hit real bad in the legs! I think he's gonna lose them. It's real bad. Red took a piece of steel in the shoulder but I hear he's gonna be okay! That's why they recalled us! Top's rebuilding the commo team! The battalion CO's chopper got shot up pretty bad too! Wounded one of his staff! Word is kiss-ass Randy puked all over the inside of the chopper! They barely made it back to Tuy Hoa! Broke both skids on a hard landing!"

Dewey nodded. He felt himself grow calm; extremely calm. Watching the jungle slide away below, all traces of the grey spot seemed to melt away. He knew what he was going to do, what he had to do.

Top Greene had sent Green to the field. Top killed Green. He was going to blow Top away as soon as they landed back in the rear. He would hunt him down and cut him in half with his M-16.

Then he was going to take Top's ears.

The chopper descended onto the same pad Dewey had lifted off from only a week earlier. The giant white X grew larger and larger until it disappeared beneath the chopper's skids as they settled on the metal deck.

Dewey leapt out of the bay, turning to grab his weapon and helmet. As they disembarked the helicopter, the pilot appeared out of nowhere. Scowling, he knelt to fill out paperwork on a clipboard he rested on one thigh. Looking Dewey right in the eyes, he started bitching as he wrote. "You boonie rats cost me a day off! Every time one of you rats wants to get laid I gotta bag my ass all over the Nam—"

Without thinking, Dewey had shoved the muzzle of his weapon in the pilot's face, locking and loading.

The pilot looked into Dewey's eyes, blazing with hatred and madness borne of fatigue and extreme loss, and knew he was on the verge of death. His face drained to white ash.

Somewhere in the distance, Tree's voice was urging Dewey to stand down. It barely registered. Pressing the muzzle harder into the pilot's face, Dewey felt the grey spot shrinking again, the spots of color fading, a sense of control returning. Though he knew the chubby helicopter pilot had no idea of the events leading up to that moment, only Tree's desperate pleading had saved the man's life.

His weapon still off safe, Dewey pressed it into the flesh between the pilot's mouth and nose as he stepped forward. "A lot of good men died out there yesterday." Dewey spat, emotion cracking his words. "It's just too fucking bad you weren't one of them."

He shoved the trembling pilot over backwards, hard, with the muzzle, then took off running across the sand on wooden planks leading to the 4th Bat's HHC row of wooden offices.

He kicked open Top's door on a dead run. The door smashed into the wall, rebounding to smash into off Dewey's shoulder as he burst in, weapon at the ready.

"You! You fuckin' sonuvabitch! I'm going to blow your skinny ass to hell! You killed him, you bastard!"

Papers flew as First Sergeant Greene recoiled from his desk, mouth agape, eyes wide open. "Wait! Wait! Who did I kill?" Top's eyes were glued on Dewey's weapon.

"Green! He should of gone home months ago. But you stuck him in LBJ and now he's dead 'cause you, you fuckin' scumbag, you sent him out there. Why not one of your ass-kissers? Why not yourself?"

Shaking with rage, Dewey advanced slowly until the muzzle of his M-16 quivered just two feet from Top's belly. Only Top's desk separated the two men.

"Now hold it! Hold it right there!"

There was no fear in Top's voice. Dewey felt cheated. He had wanted Top to beg.

"I only just now got back from the hospital. I had to look them in the face. I had to be the one to positively ID that boy Green and all the others. You think I enjoyed seeing his brains? You won't believe this, but I liked that boy! And yes, I know he was in on gassing my hooch, and you know it too, Dewey."

Top lowered his voice, but not his eyes. He raised his arms out wide from his sides in a prolonged, exaggerated shrug. His eyes held no hint of fear. "As far as his going to jail, he did that to himself. I didn't send him to jail; that wasn't my job. But I would've. He fucked up and got caught and he paid the price. I didn't have to send him out to 522 either. Ask your buddies. He volunteered when he heard it was your company involved. They all did."

Dewey slowly lowered his weapon, suddenly aware he wasn't going to kill anybody. Something in Top's voice caused him to back off mentally; Top looked older, haggard, diminished in some way. He felt the grey spot returning, tingling. He felt the threat of tears and knew he had to get out of there. He was vaguely aware of the obese supply sergeant, a .45 trained on him with both hands, belly-flopped on a desk in the other room.

Dewey abruptly turned his back on them and left. The screen door banged shut behind him.

Top didn't call out, nor did he try to have him stopped.

Dewey stood just outside the door on the boardwalk, noting the Korean's boot still nailed to the door frame.

It looked like an old story, absolutely meaningless.

He choked back a hot gush in his throat and squinted up at the sun, making rainbows with the moisture threatening to spill from his eyes. I'm a paratrooper, and paratroopers don't cry.

He didn't. Trudging through the hot sand, he made his way over to the large hooch he'd left an eternity before. Finding an empty bunk, he rolled the bare mattress out and flopped down heavily. Sleep came with merciful swiftness.

He dreamed he was with Karen, decorating the door to his freshman homeroom. She was laughing, those Cleopatra eyes sparkling under dark lashes.

November 8th, 1968

Tuy Hoa, 4th Battalion/173d's rear area

Dewey awoke soaked in sweat, a Karen dream fragmenting and dissipating as his mind groped to remember. Bluebottle flies crawled over his face, buzzed in a small cloud over his bunk. Red sat on his cot, one arm in a sling, his good hand still resting gently on the shoulder that he'd shaken Dewey awake with.

"How ya gonna be, trooper?" Red asked softly, a hint of a smile in his eyes. "Heard you guys had it pretty rough out there."

"Kinda," Dewey answered groggily, noting someone had removed his boots while he'd slept. "I heard it wasn't a picnic up on the summit either."

Their heads nodded in unison, but their eyes looked away.

"Tree told me about Green and the others." Dewey reached for a canteen and took a long drink of the piss-warm water. "Still can't believe it. It's like a bad dream. So many dead…it just don't seem possible."

His voice trailed off, leaving an awkward silence as he sat up. Red stood so he could swing his legs off the cot. "Ain't no dream." Red winced, clutching at his shoulder. "But they aren't all dead. Frenchy can have visitors now."

"Shit. Impossible, they only brought the wounded in yesterday."

"You've slept through a yesterday." Red grinned. "This here's tomorrow. Come on, let's get you out of them bloody fatigues and find ya a shower. Them pretty nurses over at the Air Force hospital won't let you through the door looking like that. And I, uh, 'borrowed' a jeep, so transportation waits. They got a lot of guys in the wards from Alpha Company, too. Except the real bad wounded. They kept Frenchy here for surgery. The rest, they've already been flown to Japan."

"Come on, Dew, let's do this."

A nurse stopped them outside the intensive care ward. She told them the doctors were with Frenchy right then, but they should come back in a few minutes.

The big, open wards were a different story. Dewey figured half of A Company was gathered around several bunks. The '60 gunner with the leg wound was sitting up in one of the beds recounting his fight with the NVA .30-cal gunner at the woodline.

Dewey stopped to talk with most of them. Suggs, and some of the other badly wounded, had already been shipped to Japan. He noticed Ding, his arm in traction with steel rods piercing the cast, lying in a bed against the far wall. Leaving the troopers of A Company to relive the battle in their excited, almost jubilant conversation, he walked over to Ding's bedside.

"*Chow uhm*, Ding. How ya feeling?"

The ex-NVA's face was contorted with pain. He nodded toward the arm. "Beaucoup oww, beaucoup oww," he repeated, shaking his head, waving Dewey away.

The American nurse that had just paged them now led them into the isolation ward. "He's very weak," she cautioned in a tone unreceptive to any argument. "Do not excite him. You can stay only five minutes. No more."

Feeling out of place in the antiseptic ward, they approached Frenchy's bed. It was easy to spot. Frenchy lay with his back to them under sheets so white they glowed. Flat white sheets. Sheets that stayed flat right up to Frenchy's buttocks. Whatever doubt, whatever hope Dewey had held onto was swept harshly away.

Frenchy had no legs. Hell, Frenchy only had half an ass!

"Frenchy? Frenchy, it's Dewey. Can you hear me, brother?"

Frenchy rose up from his pillow, craning his neck to look him in the face. Dewey felt the familiar shock, the helplessness. Frenchy's eyes were two black holes flowing with tears. He looked dead. "They butchered me, man," he managed to say in a weak voice that crackled with emotion. "They butchered me."

He turned away from them as he sank back into his pillow. Silent sobs racked what was left of his body.

The two young troopers stood next to Frenchy's bed for several empty minutes. There was absolutely nothing they could do or say. *What would it be?* thought Dewey. *"Oh, don't worry, man. They will grow back?"* When the realization of their helplessness sank in, as if by silent agreement, they turned together and walked away without a goodbye as Frenchy sobbed into his pillow.

It was late afternoon when they crossed the wire into La Bah. Tiger was there to greet them, along with the usual band of street urchins.

"I hear there big fight in mountains." Tiger said loudly, hugging Dewey's leg. "Green! He die! I 'fraid you die too, Boot!"

Looking down at his small friend, Dewey could see the kid's relief was genuine. That warmed him immensely. He reached down to scoop Tiger up in the crook of his free arm. He looked the boy in the eye and smiled. "Naww, Boot will never die on you, Tiger. Boot is a Sky Soldier! Number fuckin' one Sky Soldier. I won't die, I promise."

"Sky Soldier can die, too, Boot. Everyone...he can die, Boot," Tiger said softly, looking away.

Dewey didn't answer. He tucked Tiger's head onto a shoulder and stalked into the village.

Frenchy's whore stumbled up to them as they approached the porch of Mama-San's East. She looked a mess, sobbing and wailing and reeking of beer. Eyes glistening, she grabbed Dewey's shirt, her face a mannequin of grief. For an instant Dewey thought he'd been wrong about her, that she really did care about Frenchy. But the grief turned out to be for herself.

"Frenchy! He fini here!" she cried, slurring her words as she drew her hand in a slashing motion across her thighs. "He no marries me now. You marry me? Frenchy fini. You take me back America?"

Dewey shoved her away, hard, setting Tiger down gently as Frenchy's whore recovered and rushed him again. This time his shove sent her sprawling several feet in the sand. Tiger, aided by a few of his street gang, gently tugged her to her feet and away toward the shadows under the banyan trees, trying to soothe her in soft Vietnamese. It wasn't working.

Her wailing filled the village.

Chai Co met him at the door in a rush. No teasing or joking this time. Her eyes had met his as he mounted the first step, and she flung herself across the room to meet him in the doorway with a fierce hug. Mama-san stood just inside, her grey head bobbing with restrained emotion. Tears streamed down her face as she hurried over to kiss Dewey's cheek.

"We all hear, already. Beaucoup bad time for Sky Soldiers! Bad time VC, too!" She took one of his hands and squeezed. "You hokay, Baby-san?"

"I'm fine, Mama-san. But I need to get beaucoup dinky dow. *Ihng hue toy.* Beaucoup dinky dow!"

Seeing the pain in his eyes, she squeezed her eyes and smiled, releasing his hand. "I miss Green, too much! He make much yak-yak Vietnam. We yak much time, but no more. Never. But my Baby-san's hokay! Tonight, no charge! I souvenir you! Send Tigah for O-jays! You like?"

"Yes, Mama-san," Dewey said, stroking Chai Co's hair, feeling the warm wetness of her tears on his neck.

Late into the night, Dewey, Red, and several other troopers smoked the little, baseball bat-looking opium-treated joints. Chai Co and other whores kept them supplied with ice-cold Cokes.

As they smoked, Red filled him in on the events atop 522. How the commo team had just dismounted the Hueys and been engrossed in watching the battle rage below. How they'd felt safe as the Chinook hovered with the 4.2-inch mortar tube, and how that feeling was shattered by the incoming mortars that bracketed the summit. How there was no place to hide, no cover. Circus Boy had died instantly, a mortar round exploding at his feet. Iceman and Frenchy had dived behind some small rocks; only Iceman's head and Frenchy's legs had stuck out. How Green took a large chunk of shrapnel in the forehead. How Red himself had felt the bite of hot steel as he dove over the lip of 522's dirt-rock summit. How Green had still been alive and struggling to stand on his shattered legs in an effort to reach the departing chopper, and how he did not die until placed on the medevac. About the others, some troopers of Third Platoon riddled where they lay. The wounded. The screaming.

Dewey told of the big Indian, Santiago, now called Blue, and how the gunships had raked them on the trail. He relived the whole ordeal in minute detail, omitting only the parts about the grey spot still tingling from his head down through his limbs and his confrontation with Top.

The fear returned as he spoke. A quivering note, like a high-pitched tuning fork, set his nerves to vibrating. He felt himself sweating profusely. The grey spot quivered.

Chai Co sat at his feet, listening attentively, moving only to fetch a Coke, or to light a joint or cigarette.

A pretty new whore had also been listening, her head resting on Red's lap. Now she rose slowly, tugging gently at Red's good arm.

"You want make boom boom?" she coaxed.

"Sure. I want," Red sighed. "Only you take top."

Red groaned as the young girl helped him rise from the depths of the bamboo recliner.

Dewey watched the two stagger off into the dark hallway leading to the bedrooms. Everything seemed tinged with gold, and soft velvety shadows flickered in lamplight. Opium and marijuana flowed through his mind like warm honey. He couldn't remember ever feeling more relaxed or secure. The grey spot was almost gone. He was just fine, everything was fine, and Chai Co was helping him to his feet.

"We're paratroopers, you know," he proclaimed as she struggled to keep him from leaning too far one way or the other. To him, it was the floor that swayed, raising high on one side then slowly sinking as the other rose higher and higher. "Didja ever hear our song? No? Well. Let me enlighten you."

He started singing the paratrooper song, very loud and far off key: "THERE WAS BLOOD UPON THE RISERS! THERE WAS BLOOD UPON HIS 'CHUTE! HIS INTESTINES WERE A-DANGLING FROM HIS PARATROOPER BOOTS!"

"Shhh." Chai Co cautioned, steering him down the narrow hallway into a tiny cubicle. Her lamp spilled inky, knee-deep shadows that washed back and forth like black waves. Dewey staggered and Chai Co grasped him tighter around the waist as she lowered him to the bamboo mat.

Dewey blew out the lamp, laughing as total darkness replaced the honey gold of the flame. Chai Co hurried over to a tiny vanity, lighting a candle in front of a large, oval mirror.

He watched her image in the mirror. Lit by candlelight, she appeared to him the most beautiful woman in the world.

Suddenly vertigo swept him and twenty tiny images of Chai Co began revolving in the mirror, each held a softly glowing candle.

He squeezed his eyes shut, fighting waves of something not unlike extreme seasickness.

"AND THE MEDIC SAID, YES I HEARD HIM SAYYYYY! THAT HE AIN'T GONNA JUMP NO MORE!" He finished the Airborne Song, thinking: *and you ain't getting laid tonight, Dewey ol' boy*, as waves of what felt like hot syrup flowed over his brain like the breaking of a dam.

He felt himself slipping away as Chai Co turned from the vanity and approached the bed. He felt his body sinking, growing heavier, far too heavy to move even a finger. He forced one eye half open as Chai Co knelt to remove his boots.

"You are so very beautiful in candle light." he said from inside an elaborate sigh.

She didn't answer or look up as she undid his laces and tugged one boot free, immediately going to work on the other. His eye closed and he sank deeper, hearing his boot thump to the floor just before Chai Co gently tugged at his weapon.

"No!" he barked, clutching his M-16 close to his chest.

Kneeling next to the bed, Chai Co leaned forward, resting her cheek on his shoulder. Still fighting sleep, he could feel the warmth of tears soaking through his shirt. Softly she began singing a song in lilting Vietnamese.

He couldn't place any of the words.

He struggled to open his eyes, to reach out, to stroke her hair. He could not. He was paralyzed, stoned, and crashing big time. She knelt next to him for what seemed a long time, singing her soft song and crying.

Her fingers began gently stroking his hair as her song ceased.

"Deway?" she whispered, gently shaking his shoulder. "Deway? You wake?"

He tried to answer but could not. He could hear, but not speak; feel, but not touch.

Still stroking his hair, Chai Co began to speak, like a concerned parent to a deathly ill child. "Deway, you go back America. You no can win here. You go back America, Deway, 'fore you die too. You no can win here."

No! We're American paratroopers! We can win, we will win! They've never beaten us. They never will. We're paratroopers! American paratroopers!

No longer capable of speech, he shouted the words inside his head.

Chai Co heard nothing.

"Please, you go home. I love you, Deway. But everyone VC here. You go home to baseball, girl friend, you go home...alive. Everybody VC here. Papa-san VC...Mama-san VC...Baby-san VC."

He was slipping into the abyss when a sob shook her and he felt her lean close to his face, the softness of her lips on his cheek, the warmth of her breath in his ear. The hot splash of a tear on his neck; her soft words as she whispered into his ear:

"Deway." She paused a moment. "Deway...*I* VC."

He awoke with a start back in his hometown. It was very dark and he was lying in tall grass along the railroad tracks where he'd played soldier as a child. He had no idea how he got there, nor did he harbor any doubt that he really was home. He raised himself up on his elbows, M-16 at the ready, and looked around. His small town had been leveled. All the houses were reduced to smoldering heaps of rubble. Small flames licked around piles of shattered bricks, and soft popping sounds followed them. He had only his uniform and his M-16.

Rising to his feet, he crept onto the broken asphalt of a familiar side street. *This is insane*, he thought in a rush of panic.

The only building still standing was the P&C food market on a nearby corner. Dewey had worked there the summer he was sixteen. Now all the plate glass windows were gone, replaced with pink stucco pocked with thousands of bullet impact scars.

He felt he must go there. There was no place else. He moved in a crouch, turning this way and that, weapon at the ready to meet any threat. On the corner next to a bent and twisted street sign, two legs protruded from a pile of bricks, a child's legs, clad in ragged blue jeans, a red sneaker on one foot, a white one on the other. The legs did not move. Climbing the pile, he grasped the child's legs, pulled them toward him; then he was falling backwards. The legs in his hands were attached to nothing under the bricks. He landed hard on his back, screaming as he scrambled to his feet, knocking the child's legs away.

Lurching to his feet, he ran toward the P&C, a trip across the parking lot that seemed to take hours. There were steel doors in the back leading into the butcher shop, he remembered from the summer he had worked there. Exhausted and confused, he finally reached the doors. They were much larger than he recalled and he struggled to open them. As they swung open, a wide slice of bright white light escaped and as the doors opened wider he could see row on row of glowing, white-sheeted hospital beds.

A young anguished trooper sat up in each, screaming: "They butchered me, man! They butchered me!"

Huge, grotesquely deformed doctors hopped through several feet of blood and body parts carrying syringes the size of M-60s. Blood poured out around his legs, amputated limbs roiled in the gore pouring forth, the current forcing him back, and then boiling over him as it sucked him under and swept him away. He held his breath for as long as he could...then he had to breathe in.

He sat up gasping in total darkness. The only sound was his heart pounding in his ears and his own heavy breathing. Frantically he groped for his weapon.

It lay next to him.

Chai Co was nowhere to be seen. His bandoleer of ammo lay on the floor next to his boots. Swinging his legs off the bed, he reached down and dragged on his boots, not wasting time tying them. Fear tingled in the grey spot, spreading an icy sensation through his extremities.

Dewey had no idea how much time had passed, but he knew exactly where he was. Slinging his bandoleer and grabbing his weapon, he slipped out of the small room into the hall and flattened against the wall. As his eyes adjusted, he checked all the little side rooms.

No one anywhere; no whores, no Mama-san, no troopers. *Mama-san VC. Everyone VC.* Snapping the rifle's safety off, he slipped out onto the porch.

No one anywhere. No dogs barking. No troopers looking to get laid. No kids.

Something was very wrong.

The village lay still in silver moonlight. Not a single lamp glowed in any window. And where were the kids?

"Everyone VC. Deway, everyone VC."

That's what she'd said.

He eyeballed the opening in the barbed wire, two hundred meters away across open, moonlit sand. His eyes probed shadows under the trees and around nearby houses and shacks, finding nothing but shadows.

Maybe I'm still dreaming! he thought.

But he knew this was no dream. His heart beat hard against his ribs and the grey zone spread deeper into the marrow of his bones. His legs felt very weak, light, not his. Little dots of color danced in front of his eyes as he fought back against the grey spot. Leaning against the whorehouse wall, he sought to draw on the other place within him. The thing that allowed him to jump from airplanes, to run through machine gun fire, to want to fight in a war he truly did not, could not fully understand.

He understood now, though.

He was alone in La Bah. And either Chai Co had been telling the truth, or MPs might be cruising the village. He listened for anything that might sound like the whine of a jeep.

All he heard was the soft hush of waves on the beach. Taking a deep breath, he launched himself from the porch in full flight toward and through the break in the wire. He didn't stop running until he was almost to the barracks.

Thousands of red tracers spewed from the Korean encampment. By reflex, he dove into the sand. Red tracers. All outgoing, silent because light was so much faster than sound.

He was on his feet when the grinding of hundreds of automatic weapons arrived, engulfed him, and then transfixed him. The sound continued several seconds after the last of the tracers winked off over the rice paddies. The grey place vibrated with paranoia.

Even just walking felt strangely difficult.

He thought he heard a soft voice coming from inside the hooch as he gently opened the screen door with a loud creak. The only sounds were snores coming from various bunks, and the screen door slapping shut behind him.

Red lay on his back across one, fully clothed, his arm still in a sling.

With no warning, soft music began to drift down from the rafters, like snow. Sweet, soft repetitious music that sounded vaguely familiar. He recognized the Beatles but the song was new to him, "Hey Jude", and it seemed to go on forever in a pleasurable repetitive kind of way.

The FNG sleeping in Green's bed was black. In the bunk below, that used to belong to the Iceman, another replacement slept.

He was lily-white.

It was too much. Dewey started laughing, slowly sliding down a center support pole until he was sitting on the sandy plywood floor. The whole thing was a joke, especially this. Tears streamed down his face as he hugged his chest and his eyes flicked from Green's bunk back to Iceman's. *They'd have loved this!* He doubled up, desperately trying to keep his laughter inside.

Visions of broken, shattered dead bodies mixed with images of home. He thought of Karen and found he couldn't care anymore.

There was nothing left inside to feel anything but this new pain.

Somewhere between the words and the music his laughter died. Sucked into the grey place. Reincarnated as sobs that forced themselves from the depths of his chest as he drew into a fetal position on the floor and the song went on and on and on.

He didn't even think about paratroopers not being allowed to cry. He just let the song take him and he cried bitterly for all of them. For all the bloody ponchos with boots sticking out. For the Karen he would never have and the Chai Co he never did. For himself and all the months he had left to do in this place. For the knowledge, deep inside, that he would return to the jungles. That he did not give a shit about medals. That he would kill every VC and NVA he could ferret out of their stinking holes. That he hurt in a way he never imagined he could.

If anyone heard, they didn't show it as Dewey melted deeper into the floor, sobbing helplessly as the music covered him.

Somewhere, close by in the virgin dawn, a gecko lizard cursed loudly.

Dewey squeezed himself tighter as he rolled over onto his back and stared up at Green's radio.

"Hey Jude." The song seemed to go on forever. The taste of salt trickled into the corners of his mouth as he mimed the lizard, like the song, alternating with the lizards in cursing the virgin dawn …. over and over and over.

"Fuck You!" … Phuck yaou!... "Fuck you!"... Phuck yaou!"

The End...of a Beginning.

Glossary

For those not there:

—AK-50:drum-fed version of AK-47

—ARVN:Army of the Republic of Vietnam, articulated "AR-vin"; South Vietnamese regular soldiers

—blood wings:first wings awarded to US paratroopers, customarily smacked onto the chest so that the tack points pierced the flesh

—boonie rats:any forward US troops

—C-4:plastic explosives

—C-rations:canned food for American troops

—CA:aerial Combat Assault

—CAR-15:short version of the M-16 with folding stock, usually only carried by officers

—Charlie:the communist enemy in any form

—cherry:a new arrival in-country

—ChiCom:Chinese Communist-made, i.e. in the "People's Republic" of China

—Claymore:a remotely triggered mine firing a devastating conical pattern of steel balls

—CQ:Charge of Quarters; in practice, guarding the barracks—a duty assignment for a specified time

—CS:tear gas

—DEROS:Date of Expected Return from Overseas Separation—the date when one would be due to go home

—dust-off: Hueys used as air ambulances; also medevac

—ETA:Expected (or Estimated) Time of Arrival

—fat-rat:gallon-capacity bladder-type canteen

—FNG:Fucking New Guy; anyone new in-country, also a "cherry"

—FO:artillery forward observer; soldier trained to call in fire support

—four-deuceM-30 4.2" (106.7mm) mortar, an indirect fire support weapon heavier than the more common, easier-carried 81mm mortars organic to infantry units

—FSB:artillery Fire Support Base guarded by line troops, also called a firebase

—HE:High Explosives (generally distinguished from variants of Armor Piercing munitions; HE was minimally useful against tanks but great against troops, whereas AP was useless against troops but great against armor and fortifications)

—Herd or The Herd:nickname for the 173d Airborne Brigade

—hoochany basic dwelling from barracks to a poncho tent or even a bamboo hut

—Hub:an area in South Vietnam where five rivers met, forming a pattern like the spokes of a wheel on maps (or as seen from above), outside of Tuy Hoa

—in-country:if your boots were on the ground anywhere in Vietnam, you were serving "in-country"

—LAW:M-72 Light Anti-Tank Weapon often used in firefights to neutralize bunkers, US version of the RPG; a handheld, disposable 66mm weapon that succeeded the WWII and Korean War bazooka

—LBJ:Long Binh Jail; a stockade in which errant US soldiers did time

—lifer: anyone making a career of the Army, especially in sweet gigs requiring little risk or effort

—lurps:freeze-dried, high-energy rations, often with rice as the main ingredient as in beef and rice, chicken and rice, etc; issued to frontline personnel (especially Long Range Reconnaissance Patrols, hence LRRPs, articulated as "lurps") who could prepare hot meals by boiling water in canteen cups using chunks of C4 and pouring the water into the pouches

—LZ:Landing Zone

—medevac:helicopter used in medical evacuation, a.k.a. "dustoff"

—MPC:Military Payment Certificate; also called scrip, issued in place of US Dollars as pay; a weapon against black market activity

—NVA:North Vietnamese Army

—P-38:Army-issue can opener included with C-rations, about two inches long

—PRC-25:the AN/PRC-25 man-portable military radio, also called the "prick"

—The Real World:the USA, a.k.a. The World

—Red leg:US Army Artillery (for the service branch color; infantry, for example, is teal blue—this is why you see yellow stripes on pants in old cavalry movies, as cavalry's branch color was/is yellow)

—ROK:Republic of Korea (South Korean troops); normally articulated spelled out "are-oh-kay"

—RPG:Rocket-Propelled Grenade, an anti-armor weapon also useful against infantry and especially fortifications; in Vietnam this typically meant the Soviet-designed RPG-7

—RTO:Radio Telephone Operator—the soldier who carried the PRC-25

—Shithook:CH-47 Chinook; large double-rotor helicopter used to transport troops and equipment

—SOP:Standard Operating Procedure; what troops are expected to do without having to be told

—VC:Viet Cong; communist guerrilla fighters of South Vietnam, called by themselves the "National Liberation Front"

—ville:any small Vietnamese town

—Willie Peter (WP):white phosphorus, a munition that ignites in contact with air, creating green fire, dense white smoke; causing agonizing skin burns

National Veterans Foundation

Following his return from Vietnam in 1971, Shad Meshad started the Vietnam Veterans' Re-Socialization Unit at the Brentwood, California VA hospital, the first unit of its kind in the United States. He spent the next eight years in the Los Angeles area working with Vietnam veterans and their severe readjustment problems. He successfully lobbied and educated the Veterans Administration and the Congress on his program. In 1979, Shad pioneered the nationwide Vietnam Vet Center Outreach Program and became the Regional Director for the western United States. He served for seven years in the development of this national program. This became an important program of veterans helping veterans.

In November 1985, Shad Meshad took it a step further when he founded the Vietnam Veterans Aid Foundation. This successful organization, renamed the National Veterans Foundation in May 1992 due to its expanded services to all veterans, presently serves over 150,000 veterans and dependents each year. The foundation is a non-profit, non-political organization whose purpose is to continue the process of rehabilitating and integrating American veterans into productive roles in mainstream society. This mission is achieved through public education, individual referral, crisis intervention, and professional education and training.

Funds raised and grants received by the Foundation are allocated to the most qualified direct service organizations throughout the nation. Additionally, the foundation assists veterans and their families by targeting projects and studies in these areas:

- Homelessness

- Post-Traumatic Stress Disorder (PTSD)

- Chemical and Alcohol Dependence

- Job Training and Placement

- POW/MIA Resolutions

To learn more about vets helping vets, please contact the National Veterans Foundation, a 501(c)3 recognized organization, at 5757 West Century Blvd, Suite #350, Los Angeles, CA 90045.

About the Author

Vernon E. Brewer II is a 70-year-old multiple Purple Heart recipient and Vietnam Veteran who was raised in Seneca Falls, New York and now resides deep in the Finger Lakes National Forest. He left Seneca Falls for the US Army, training as a paratrooper, before going to Vietnam in early spring of 1968—which would otherwise have been his senior year of high school.

Raised in a small town with plenty of patriotism and a philosophy of "my country, right or wrong," Verne grew up reading Sergeant Rock comic books and thought he was off to prove himself to everyone back home. Not being a part of the in-crowd at school, and being the naive teenager that he was, he pictured himself coming home a war hero. In his mind this would gain him great respect and status from the whole community, especially the schoolmates who had looked down on him throughout his school years. And Karen Coleman would have to fall in love with him.

Before the rest of his class graduated that June without him, he was in his first real battle, had killed his first enemy soldier, and had earned the first of his three purple hearts. Needless to say, he grew up very fast in Vietnam when faced with the realities and carnage of real warfare.

Verne served eleven months in Vietnam in 1968 and 1969, a time which included some of the bloodiest fighting of the war. There was one bad week in November of 1968, which included the battle for Hill 522 that lives in his mind to this day. Later in his tour, while walking point for a small contingent of paratroopers outside An Khe, he was impaled in the thigh by a punji stick while running for cover in the midst of an ambush.

He was medevaced back to the States, where he spent nine months recuperating at Fort Devens Army Hospital. While recuperating from his wound, he received a phone call from home, informing him of bad news. The beautiful young girl he had gone to Vietnam hoping to impress, Karen Coleman, had been murdered by a 15-year-old boy who lived in her Rochester apartment building.

Shortly after being released from the hospital, Verne was reintroduced to a pretty girl he had met just before leaving for Vietnam. They married and had two children, but Verne was restless and moved all around the country looking for himself and the America of his visions of home while serving in Vietnam. He never seemed to find that America until he returned home to Seneca County, New York. The marriage did not last, but he has kept in contact with his children and today enjoys them as young adults.

During this period of his life, Verne decided that the only way he was ever going to put aside the memories and dreams of the really bad side of the experience in Vietnam was to write. The vivid memories that had festered in his mind ever since Vietnam were with him constantly, awake or asleep. He came to believe the only way he could put those memories to rest was to write about it. It took years of fighting grief, nightmares, and intrusive memories to finish the manuscript.

Even still, he never thinks he has done justice to those memories.

Meanwhile, he went back to school. At Cayuga Community College he was elected president of the student body in his senior year and graduated with an Associate's Degree in Humanities and Social Sciences.

He then matriculated to Brockport (SUNY) State University, where he worked toward dual degrees in deviant psychology and English creative writing. It was at Brockport that the early drafts of this book won the 1983 Writer's Forum Scholarship.

During his time at Brockport, the author took a four-month hiatus from his studies to ride a Harley-Davidson motorcycle around the country, sky-diving in the company of other veterans, to bring attention to problems the Vietnam veterans were experiencing due to exposure to Agent Orange. He traveled to nearly every state and major city, skydiving in each city to build public awareness of this terrible tragedy. The trip, code-named Sunset Orange, made Agent Orange a household word.

While touring in Los Angeles he met Shad Meshad, who had created the concept of Vietnam Veteran Outreach Centers which grew into the National Veterans Foundation. Verne became interested in the Foundation and its concept that vets can help themselves and each other, as they did in Vietnam, rather than depending on the government to provide assistance for them. He has been an enthusiastic supporter ever since.

All the author's royalties from this book's first edition were given to the National Veterans Foundation to help them help Vets. A large portion of the royalties from the second printing was donated to the Sky Soldier Memorial Fund at Fort Benning, Georgia.

Verne Brewer now lives alone in an A-frame tucked way back into the Finger Lakes National Forest and rides with the Vietnam Vets / Legacy Vets Motorcycle Club.